Cathy O Malley was born in the West of Ireland and grew up listening to the music of Motown, Rock and Roll and seventies music.

The author travelled to the Middle East with her family in the late 1980s and early '90s and experienced first-hand the Gulf War from her home close by the military airbase there.

She lives in The West of Ireland with her dog, Rover!

For Mike and Cid.

Cathy O Malley

...ON A DONKEY
CALLED ELVIS

AUSTIN MACAULEY PUBLISHERS™

LONDON • CAMBRIDGE • NEW YORK • SHARJAH

A CIP catalogue record for this title is available from the British Library.

ISBN 9781035809400 (Paperback)
ISBN 9781035809417 (ePub e-book)

www.austinmacauley.com

First Published 2023
Austin Macauley Publishers Ltd®
1 Canada Square
Canary Wharf
London
E14 5AA

I would like to acknowledge the team at Austin Macauley Publishers.

I would like to thank my family for being so encouraging always and my good friends:

Annette, Eileen, Dawn, Claire and Mel… and many more… you know who you are.

Chapter 1

My name is Cathy. I am a child of the sixties and I had a fairly unremarkable childhood. But when I was seventeen, the bottom fell out of my world. My brother Morgan was killed in a road traffic accident. That was a profound life changing experience. Whereas I had been your ordinary teenager trying to navigate the uncharted waters of adolescence, as unmemorable as it is for most people, suddenly everything changed. I was man overboard. Or woman overboard. I am not a swimmer.

That was in 1976, and it is the first episode in my life that I have total recall of that hurt so much. Well, that's not quite accurate, this was the event which was the longest blur of my life and yet I recall everything so vividly even though it happened some forty odd years ago. I was devastated. We were all devastated. My family and I. That incident reshaped my life thereafter. Euphemistically speaking, I had to learn quickly to swim, or drown.

Swim or drown.

Sink or swim!

Sink or swim?

Swim I suppose.

You see what happened was, we were at my oldest brother's wedding when 'it' happened. What a day we all had had?

Even my mother was there and she left the house for a whole day. That was something.

She had M.S. or some kind of similar condition which the doctors hadn't named yet. Including herself, everyone thought she had arthritis. Anyway arthritis or M.S. or whatever ailed her kept her housebound for much of my life once I had turned eight. Nothing would move her too far from her front door. For her, her life was over. It was about being invalided. Not mobile. One day: amazingly agile, the next day: Sedentary.

It made me miserable, mostly, but on Nick's wedding day, I had an escape for a short while from the hard reality of my mother's ailment.

I have to say I was blissfully happy that day, I was gaining a sister-in-law. To me this was pure joy. I lived in anticipation for months ever since they announced their engagement. I couldn't wait for the day they walked back down the aisle together and I could say then I have a sister-in-law. I happily ignored the 'in-law' bit. And Nula was some female relief in an otherwise male populated world. I never resented being an only girl. It had its advantages. A strong sense of self in a male dominated world would come in handy down through the years.

So as I was the only girl in a family of seven, I needed the company of another female and with good reason obviously. My six brothers had probably six close friends so I had no shortage of male company. Not a bad start in life if I may say so. But not because it turned me into some sort of slut or a flirt, it's just that I was used to men, even though they were not used to me. It served me well to live in a predominantly 'males rulc the world', world.

I cope nicely in male-driven spheres. Men in power do not phase me. Thankfully.

Good for me.

But I'm still a teenage girl remember, with teenage girl angst.

I likened myself down through the years to Megan Cleary, the heroine of the *Thornbirds*, written by the Antipodean author, Coleen Mc Cullough. Or maybe I couldn't get her story out of my head since it and my story bear many similarities.

That story was fiction. My story is fact. Barring having an affair with a Cardinal of the church, and a child by him, mine is fairly tame.

Anyway, the day of Nick's wedding to Nula had gone really well and some of us had relocated to the local dancehall to round off the night's festivities, because weddings did not go on so long in those days. They ended with the couple leaving for their honeymoon at about eleven o'clock. And the guests were usually expected to just disperse.

I loved dancing and still do. I was with my friends laughing, and enjoying the showband, as I recall, probably that ill-fated group, The Miami, when my brother Sid came to get me.

'Cathy, Morgan's been in an accident,' he breathlessly informed me.

'When?

Where?

How?'

11

'He was coming back into town after closing the pub. He was close to home when the accident happened.'

We had a family run public house back in those days and it was not customary to close, ever, except for Christmas Day and Good Friday, so we had hired staff that day to cover for us but someone in the family had to cash up and close up. Morgan was the logical choice. He was familiar with the chore and the most clued in, having worked oftener there than any of the rest of us, barring Nick, who was manager.

'Where is he?'

'In the intensive care unit at the hospital.'

'How did this happen?' I asked as I grabbed my jacket from the cloakroom, which thankfully was quiet at that stage, and followed him out the door.

He didn't have any information himself so we were hoping it wasn't serious.

Later, it was revealed the car he was travelling in was struck head on by a drunk driver. Morgan's non-drinking girlfriend, Holly, was driving. They had volunteered to leave the wedding early to lock up shop and planned to re-join the rest of us afterwards to dance the night away at the most popular dancehall for miles around, Club Armitage.

In those days there was no such thing as a seat belt. Well, there was but they mostly went unused and there was no rule to enforce their use. Cars were generally slower and speed wasn't an issue. And drinking and driving regulations had just been introduced and loosely enforced at that time.

My brother Morgan was on life support for four days.

I loved him so much.

We all did.

We hugged him.

We kissed him.

We begged him to wake up.

We prayed for him. We waited and we waited.

We hoped against hope.

He didn't look at all bad. His face was unscathed and still beautiful.

Apart from the tubes sticking into him and hanging out of him, he looked quite fine.

Rather like someone asleep.

They were giving us time though.

The doctors.

To come to terms with the inevitable.

And for the second time that week my mother left the house, to visit her beautiful brain-dead son in the hospital.

We coped through those mind-numbing days as best we could. We communicated with each other in short clipped sentences.

Are you ok?

Is Mammy okay?

Is Daddy okay?

How will we ever survive this? Conversation seemed to be useless and unnecessary. We all felt the same.

Helpless.

We shuffled around the hospital in a daze. We inhaled slowly. We exhaled heavily. As if every breath was our last. As if we were underwater and the oxygen in our oxygen tanks was quickly running out. We didn't sleep. We clung to one another for support even though as time went on, we each knew there was no way back for him. It dawned on all of us at different times during those few terrible days that there was something awful happening to us and we had absolutely no control over it.

And no defence against the attack that had assaulted us.

If only there was some way back…For Morgan.

For the rest of us. But you can't turn back the clock. The axe had fallen already.

We begged God.

We cursed God.

We maligned God.

We denied the existence of God.

But we had to depend on God to keep us going. We were Catholics so we had to follow the only route of hope afforded to us.

There was no other way to survive the shock and pain and terror of what was happening to all of us. A loved one we had lived with and grown up with as children and young adults was on the point of going away permanently. Never to be seen, touched, talked to, laughed with, cried with ever again.

Death is very final.

I discovered this the hard way. I didn't want to have this experience but I had no choice. I was a prisoner of reality. And I was unmoored from all that I had ever known.

I was also on the edge of whatever abyss that situation had pointed us to.

Death.

When we didn't even know yet what life was about. Like I said I was devastated.

Intensive care was on the second floor of the local hospital and we were taking turns going down to the hospital chapel to pray, which was on the ground floor. You could feel the anguish there of so many years of the prayers and hopes and the silence. What's to say? Hospital chapels are such lovely, quiet places.

Filled with hope. But they are such very sad places too.

Filled with dread. I'll always remember the atmosphere of that chapel at that time. I can feel it now as I write. Hope and dread.

Goosebumps still after all these years. As the saying goes, 'Where there's life there's hope.'

Ultimately the decision was made to turn off the life support machines on Thursday.

By my parents and a doctor in the family. After a long vigil, lasting several days, I was packed off home to bed that evening. I was, apparently, to mind my younger sibling, David, while the older ones witnessed the inevitable. And I knew exactly what was happening in my absence.

A life being switched off.

Nick, my newly married brother, came to my room that night to call me out of a fitful sleep to tell me Morgan was gone. Intuitively I knew what had happened. I cried on his shoulder for what seemed like hours. Unhappily for him he had come across the accident on the night he should have been going on his honeymoon, which was en route to his honeymoon destination and had spent every waking hour afterwards at Morgan's hospital bedside. And Nula along with him.

As the oldest, he took on that responsibility as neither my father nor my mother was capable of having a lucid thought throughout that entire time. I guess they had to be sedated.

The details of those few days and the funeral are not uncommon. Alas, most people can identify with the way funerals play out. All deaths are tragedies. This one was a disaster. It literally tore us all up emotionally and snatched us from normality and put us onto a road that none of us had chosen. We had to take on the loss of a son and sibling. What used to be a fairly normal family now had to contend with a mountain of pain and to top it all off my parents, especially my mother, were not coping. How could she, about to bury her own child?

He was too young to die. He was only eighteen. He had his whole life ahead of him.

Road deaths back in those days were uncommon so it was an even bleaker time for everyone in the community.

Why did he die?

Why him?

Why not the drunk driver, that crashed into them. He walked away unscathed.

Morgan's girlfriend had minor injuries but she was totally inconsolable. We all really felt for her. Minding her became my priority.

So we somehow managed the interminable funeral queues for two whole never-ending days. There was no choice. I wanted to run as far away from my life at that point as I could. The pain was insurmountable. Thank God for people and their support. I love people as a result. That love and support has stayed with me all my days since.

The queues at the morgue and the church on day one and the ones outside the church and in the graveyard on day two were long and tiring, but it had to be.

Funerals go on far too long I think.

But the people kept coming and coming, to sympathise. They loved him too you see. They couldn't be denied the opportunity to pay their last respects.

My father nearly passed out when the undertaker closed the casket. My mother was totally numb and, yes, she was there to say goodbye to her beloved Morgan, for both days. That ended her outings from home, for the duration of her life thereafter.

I should have been able to carry them both emotionally and God knows I wanted to.

I should have had some magic words to take the pain away from them.

If only I could get past my own.

Closed casket…lowering of coffin…finality.

The sadness and grief at that graveyard was unreal and indescribable.

I can't even begin to try to find the words to create a picture of the emotionally charged atmosphere.

Angry, black, mournful sobs all around.

Probably Seamus Heaney says it best, everyone, '…Coughed out angry tearless sighs…'

The weather in graveyards during funerals seems always to be cold and wet. This day was no exception. It matched everyone's mood. It was early May.

Back at home we had more neighbours and friends calling, all trying to buoy us up, but grief is contagious and they left us worse off than when they had come. Bless them.

People are wonderful, were wonderful.

Every funeral I go to since, I remember Morgan. I'm not much good at funerals as a result.

After a few days there's calm.

The euphoria wears off and the reality sets in. It's true when people say, '*it* hasn't hit home yet.'

Because after an unspecified number of days, 'it' kicks in. 'It' kicks and kicks and kicks some more, till you feel battered and bruised and down on the ground mentally and emotionally and physically and spiritually.

The death and the funeral are bad but the reality is shattering.

Every nerve ending in the body is so acutely aware of the pain in the heart that they immobilise a person.

You internally shout out your anguish but no sound comes out. And even though you are still surrounded by family and friends and all things familiar it's as if no one and nothing is familiar anymore. All things are strange and all people are strangers. Strangers you want to hug and cling to. Situations you want to bury yourself in and feel warmth from because they were once familiar and all you really want is for life to go back to the way it was and the person back with you because you can't cope with the pain and thankfully for a time you lose a grip on reality itself because if you didn't you would die too, of heartache.

Initially you try to do normal things. Getting up to make a cup of tea is monumental in its required effort. Your feet are leaden. Your mind is leaden. Your heart is leaden. It is so hard to move on, to go on, but go on you must.

That was a lifetime ago but it's like as if it were yesterday.

Back to my mother for a minute.

She died young and I'm glad for her sake that she did.

I'm not happy about it you understand, I was gutted when she passed away but it saved her from much of her life's hardships.

She never fully recovered from the shock she was in when Morgan died. It was her undoing. I believe he was her favourite. We were not jealous of that, but, on the contrary, we loved him all the more for it. He was everyone's favourite.

All of us.

He had a 'joie de vivre' about him even though he was in and out of hospital with medical problems and I think this is why she favoured him.

He minded everyone and his humour was infectious.

He coached me through my teenage years of crushes and sexual challenges. His lessons in the opposite sex were real and comic. The way he made me laugh in those days, I feel like a giggle now. And a tear. I miss him. But who wouldn't?

He was the tallest in the family by far and a young Elvis lookalike. Aquiline nose chiselled features, intense eyes. Dark. Handsome.

He went dancing, he went fishing, he liked to clay pigeon shoot. He finished school and got a job as a barman in a local hotel. He was due to start his new job the following Monday after the wedding but it never came to pass.

He was good at it too because he was such a cool personality behind a bar.

He had a quick wit and a lively imagination. He was an entertainer by nature. We miss not knowing what he could have achieved if he was still with us. He was certainly such a positive individual, it could only have been good. What he could have been will never be known. That's tragic. And made all the more tragic because it leaves a gap which cannot ever be filled.

He had that faraway look in his eye which can be seen in the last photo taken of him at his brother's wedding.

My newly married brother and my new sister-in-law were inconsolable. Who could blame them? What was to be the happiest day of their lives turned out to be their saddest and they are reminded of the tragedy daily.

And yes, they are still perfectly happily married if perfect happiness is possible. The closest couple I know, and the most solid, just don't mention that awful day. He is my other daddy. He minds me.

My mother malingered after that for about sixteen years in her crushed, heartbroken, unwell state. She mustered up as much courage as possible and put on a brave face every day for the rest of her life. She rallied as best she could and seemed for the most part to be normal and happy and functioning on a very stable level, but we could tell she was otherwise. Every so often the cracks would show. But she was happy and contented for the rest of us and the people she knew and loved. She sacrificed mostly any semblance of brokenness for our sake and it seemed to work for her. She busied herself with having people in the house and enjoyed company. She had always had a stoic approach to life and a sense of humour and she must have dredged up from deep within the stuff that survival is made of and an unnatural strength to live as normal as possible for the rest of her life. She died when she was seventy-two which is young by modern standards.

But like I said it saved her from further ill health and sorrow.

I miss her.

I miss my dad. He died aged ninety-four. He was a tough man. I was on my own with him when he died. I felt privileged. I was his favourite you see and the apple of his eye apparently. I turned a bit sour later on down the road in life when I was transitioning from teenager to adult. But he still loved me. Enough about my father.

I was generally, in those days, all about my mother anyway, whether it was worrying over her since Morgan died, or being frustrated at her due to her medical limitations, which wasn't her fault. My dad hardly got a look in, in my life anymore.

Anyway, my mother was around long enough to witness the death of my first husband when I was twenty-six. He died on the road as a result of a car crash, no seat belt this occasion as well. I had four children by then.

My mother was beautiful, and as a couple my mother and father were; 'Hollywood'. A very glamorous duo!

Before she married my father, she was a nurse in Scotland. She told us stories of travelling back and forth between Belfast and Stranraer during the war. When renewing her travel pass, she would get notes of proposition from the passport office. Her photos must have been so memorable. I guess single ladies with a career were sought after in those days. Typically dressed in the fashion of the day, I love looking at old photos of her and him.

A tight-fitting suit for her, relevant to the times, and always a hat.

It was considered proper for women to wear hats out of doors always. My father always wore a hat and a three-piece suit of clothes, mostly tweed or herringbone.

They were quite sartorial. That was called the 'Sunday Best'. They were less formal during the week.

She met my dad through her sister who was dating my uncle, his brother. Six weeks later mom and dad were married. The other couple split up.

My mother was a happy person and loved people even from the confines of her home. After she fell ill, she didn't want to use a wheelchair, preferring instead to stay indoors. Moving about had become a challenge to her when I was around eight or nine, as you know, and she never had therapy to alleviate the situation, if that were possible, back then.

She was a friend to everyone. She gave everyone her attention. She accepted people no matter what their flaws, with the exception, of my grandmother, a meddling old bitch who I will share about further along in my tale.

There was great nature in my mother. She was a carer, not selfish or self-centred.

Everyone loved her but not out of pity. She was such a lady. People came daily to visit her in her house. Out of the generosity of their hearts.

I remember when I was young, *very* young, she would don her suit and hat and take me to the local hospital for X-rays on my facial glands. I used to suffer from a very painful condition which they called, at the time, 'Swollen Glands,' a condition I shared with my older brother Nick. My mother and I would take the train to the city, just the two of us. We used to have a lovely day out, but my abiding memory of her from those days is the way she dressed up and made up her face and used lipstick.

(The randomness of the things we remember after years of dormancy in the mists of times past.) Well, anyway it was in stark contrast to my mother as an older woman. Disabled, confined, wearing *comfortable* clothes, to hide her disabled legs. She had great legs as I recall, I had seen them when she wore her suits and good dresses. She always put on her face and lipstick though. Fair play to her.

The movie 'Pearl Harbour,' reminds me of my mother and when I saw Kate Beckinsale in her off-duty suits and hat and very red lipstick, I thought instantly of my mother. The off duty carefree nurse. I am probably just daydreaming too.

She loved her children though and never for a moment in my entire life slipped into resentment towards us or pity for herself. If I am half the woman she was, I am happy with myself.

Like so many others in those days, my parents were good role models and they took their responsibilities as parents very seriously. There were very few distractions. Television didn't arrive in our house until I was six. They never frequented the public house and were usually too busy looking after us to do much visiting. Religious observances were the major cause of them leaving the house after six or on Sundays and other days of obligation.

They had their differences as do all couples, but they stuck with us through thick and thin, and probably had seriously hard challenges, my grandmother being top of the list.

They taught us manners and grace and instilled a sense of respect for everyone including the ever-present wagon that she was, Mother. Not Granny or Nanny or anything of a soft nature but, 'Mother.'

So that was the way it was with her, my mum. And my dad.

My father was hard working and neither one of them drank. They liked a cigarette now and again. But they did nothing to excess. In the early years, she helped him with the outdoor chores as did, and do, farmer's wives. Life on the land can be cruel and kind so there was a quiet resignation to the daily toil. He headed off to work as a foreman or 'Ganger' as it was known back then, on the local railway early in the day. He had to be up before dawn to take care of the daily, early morning work and was 'ganger' for the rest of the day, coming home tired, he faced more work on the land, but she helped him as best she could. For them, life was far from idyllic but they made the most of things and enjoyed the times when Mother went to visit her other offspring in the city.

Our citified cousins.

They had running water and toilets that flushed and a bathtub probably, while we were still out the back 'picking our own half acre.' For our night time ablutions we had the 'gerry', as we affectionately called the chamber pot. We had to take turns emptying the 'gerry' every morning and making sure it was clean for the next nights ablutions. We pulled ourselves into the twentieth century roughly around the same time of the coming of the electric light.

That was back then when life wasn't half bad. Or my youthful innocence hadn't been eroded too much by the grandmother. And other life's misfortunes.

Chapter 2

They named me after my grandmother, Catherine, first of a long and undistinguished line of widowed matriarchs.

Yes! Most of my aunts were widows in their forties.

I was never thrilled to bear *her* name. I thought it a bad omen. I thought there was a hint of disgrace to it, considering the type of person we as a family had to live with.

I've since reconciled with my parents' decision to call me after her.

I like my name now. I suppose time and space can heal any hurt. Or at least dampen it down a bit.

I have a niece bearing my name also. I am thrilled. And a grand-niece too.

My grandmother had ten children and lost her husband when her children were young. She lived for another forty years or so.

Well, long enough anyway to terrorise me, my brothers, my father and reduce my mother to a smouldering wreck.

All my cousins, the ones who didn't live with her, think she was the best thing since the sliced pan. (Bread made and pre-sliced in the bakeries. Typical Irish phrase.)

Well, maybe she was to them but she ate up my mother with her complete and utter contrariness.

Several people can't all have it wrong. We loved to see her getting onto the train across the fields heading off to the city. We let out a collective sigh of relief when she left but all inhaled deeply again on her return, only to live on tenterhooks until her next excursion away from us.

She was authoritarian, highly critical and a master busybody.

She was not widely liked around the area. Respected maybe.

She may have been admired to a certain extent, having raised such a large family. Most of her daughters went to college which was unheard of in those days. The men were expected to go out to work. They were needed to contribute to the upkeep of all the family. That was typical, I believe, in homesteads in those days. Modern times has changed all that and an earning sibling is expected to leave home and rent their own place.

To her credit, she put a lot of store in education and it rubbed off on me I think. (But only after a certain amount of dithering on my part in my late teens into my early twenties.) At least all my uncles were literate and most passed the Group Cert in secondary school. I have an abiding memory of my dad reading the daily paper each day. His greatest enjoyment outside of his family was when his Readers Digest, which he subscribed to for years, arrived in the post. He was an avid reader and had stacks of Digests in his corner near his favourite chair as her grew older. He wasn't third level educated but he had a natural curiosity about the world and he fed his brain through reading.

My grandmother stifled this gift in his life in the early days. She believed work was the only thing one needed.

Activities outside of that were
related by an older cousin of
'mart', or 'fair'. We, my famil
young or unborn at that point
called him at six, drove seve
wretched animals all day til
winter. She didn't get the pri
the frozen animals the sever
sheepdog, obviously, since there w...

In those days you
milk was sold f
for city dwe
their inco
I
pla

and farmyard entrances to avoid along the way. He got tea and
bread for his fifteen-hour day out. He was twelve at the time.
There was no chance of a fiscal reward. He was, probably
according to her, able bodied, available and a male relative,
so he should have looked on doing this job for her as a duty
and obligation.

No one walks several miles nowadays unless it's for
leisure or charity!

She was that tough and not in the positive sense of the
word.

My first memory of her, on looking back now, was that
she was so cantankerous she had no patience with me at all
and I would never forget her spitefulness towards me one
particular day. Most people remember their first day at school,
or a Christmas present, or some other nice event. This
memory of mine was so *not* nice that it overshadows all other
memories during those formative years, barring the lovely
ones I have of my mother as a young and able-bodied woman.

I was an early riser as a child. My parents, being farmers,
and working a smallholding of land, had to go out of the house
each morning at the crack of dawn to milk the cows to have it
ready for the milk lorry when it was doing milk collections.

could not buy milk in a shop. Most of the ... processing into butter and cheese or bottling ...lers. Selling milk to the creamery was part of ...me which helped to support my brothers and me.

...emember this particular morning my mother had left me ...ying with some make-up compacts she had. They were probably empty, since make up was no longer much of a priority in her life, now that she had married and had given up her job nursing.

That was the rule back then before the Reform for Equality of Women was introduced.

Thinking back now she probably couldn't spend money on such frivolities as make up as 'Mother' would deem it unnecessary. In 'Mothers' absence she would apply it and after the old lady died, she used it daily.

Anyway I was sitting happily beside a warm fire minding my own three-year-old business when she stormed into the room and took all my mother's things from me. Being too young to protest, I started to cry.

'What are you doing there with your mother's things? That stuff costs money. Clear off back to bed and don't be annoyin' me now,' were her cruel words of scolding. I've never forgotten that morning, particularly when I went crying to my mother as she came in, which started a holy row between the two women.

In most farms back in those days it was common for the heir to the farm to live with the ageing parents. I used often wish that I was one of the town cousins who didn't have to live with such a wild virago as my grandmother.

Eventually she broke her eighty-nine-year-old hip and was bedridden for several years while my own mother had to care for her till she died. Needless to say she ruled the roost and commanded obedience from all, even from the confines of her bed, till her dying day. It was so much better that her movements were restricted but she still managed to overwhelm me with her crankiness and meanness.

The only vice my mother ever had was enjoying a cigarette or two. To accomplish this she had to creep away over the fields where she wouldn't be seen. Otherwise there would be some to-do if she was discovered. The grandmother saw smoking as a waste of money. Any money she had she probably gave it to the city cousins. We never saw any of it. And my mother certainly didn't.

When I was young, before the accident that changed everything, I had a real Alice Taylor type of life (barring the 'run-ins' with the grandmother).

'To School Through the Fields' and all that. Lovely memories of a quaint, but looking back now, tainted childhood.

(It generally ended at the school gate. My Alice Taylor type lifestyle!)

Bringing the sod of turf to school to keep the fire going, to keep the schoolhouse warm in the winter, to keep the milk hot.

To keep the Master's arse warm as he stood with his back to the fire, blocking off the heat from us children. Oh well he could have done worse things. And some of them Masters did. I took to wearing pants at the age of ten. Hid my legs! I started the pants wearing revolution at school then.

That was the master.

The missus, his wife, was a total tyrant.

She was eternally scolding or whipping or ear pulling.

I don't know how we learned anything. She lay on heavy with the cane as did her husband. Lord how did we come out of school half as sane as we are is a mystery to me? Nowadays behaviour like that would see teachers incarcerated and the 'poor' student helped with several rounds of therapy.

But 'The Missus,' as we called her was good with needles. She taught us all to be capable knitters, embroiderers, seamstresses and crocheters, if there's such a word.

While the boys were out playing football.

Feck.

I wished I was out with them instead of getting the cane on the knuckles if I dropped a stitch while knitting, or if I hemmed a crooked hem. I was so good at the crafts though that for years I mended, stitched, darned and knitted for all my several brothers. She taught me well I have to say, fair play to her.

With all my brothers I would have made a better boy. We would have had a seven-a-side. So back then I was deemed a tomboy, because I played rugby and soccer and football with them and their friends in the evenings and when we had free time from farm work, which wasn't often. I liked being a tomboy. But I was never spoiled. I was the one who polished all the shoes on Saturday night for first Mass on Sunday. That kind of 'not spoiled at all.'

By natures wisdom I was too short to be a guard, an early career ambition of mine, and a girl playing Gaelic football was unheard of and was frowned on in those days.

I was ahead of my time I guess!

If it was now, I'd be 'In With the In Crowd.' (As Bryan Ferry was once noted to chant.)

I'd be deemed an 'all-star' football player and sure, size isn't an impediment nowadays to joining the police force.

Occasionally, I might make a reference to a 'Pop' star or a 'Pop' song. It's my way of saying I always loved music. I could tell you facts about music going back to the sixties. I wished too, back then, that I could have been a DJ, another 'no-no' for women, as I was growing up and maturing. And as time has gone by though we now have more female D.J.s than you could shake a stick at. A career which is widely coveted. At least by me.

So back to the task at hand.

Thankfully, I muddled my way through primary school. It didn't end soon enough.

Out of school in the evening I had to navigate my way home through the bully girls.

The ringleader was a fiery redhead and she took so much joy rounding up the other girls in our village to intimidate me or blank me depending on whichever mood she was in. To be fair to her she was a strikingly attractive girl.

Formidable though, in a raw sort of way.

She would probably be a very valuable individual in a revolution or some such. A Maud Gonne type. Statuesque and determined. I liked her a lot.

Even though I hated her. And I so wanted her to like me and not pick on me.

Sometimes she allowed the others to be nice to me, but I was always aware that she was about to pounce at any time, so I used to live life holding my breath. These control freaks are just so insecure themselves they cannot be nice since they are so fecked up that anyone who is successful or going places has to be pulled back. Which is what she thought of me; I had

31

the opposite opinion of myself mind you. And they have a ready following because their insidious twisting of the truth actually works in their favour because every peer group needs a leader and the one who can crow the loudest is usually deemed the boss.

Mindless minions, I suppose, with ridiculous ringleaders.

My liberation from her came in secondary school when she dropped out after year one, to work. Common enough practice in those days. No Education Acts back then to ensure attendance till 16 years of age.

One of the happiest days of my life thus far was when I discovered she had left school for good. But for a while I was nervous that it might have only been a ruse and that she was just off sick.

Days turned into weeks with no sign of her and then I forgot about her altogether.

I acquired a life-long friend when left to my own devices. Her name was Tina.

A great person, I have to say.

Very consistent with a sense of humour which matched my own. We learned how to smoke together. As young people do. We attended the Saturday night Youth Club and walked several miles home each night.

And she had a mother that wasn't ill, like mine, and Tina got to go places with her mother that I never went with mine. Shopping. The cinema. Days out. Getting the hair done.

I was secretly hung up about that for years but it never interfered with our friendship.

As I grew older, I took on more responsibility looking after the house.

I was good at it too. It's one of my best skills.

Housekeeping. And I like it. Second to being a mother. Third to being a wife. Fourth to being a teacher. That was in my future though.

But I was too young for that responsibility, back then, and I looked on with longing as my friends had Sunday outings, and so on, while I had to take the place of my mother. Cooking and washing and cleaning. But it was good life training if not a little restricting. And I was happy to help her.

I remember doing the washing, first with a washboard and bath and that nasty skin flailing 'carbolic' soap. 'Lifebuoy,' I think it was called but I could be wrong. Then we progressed to a machine which had a wringer to wring the water out of the clothes. Two rollers were twisted manually by a handle. It was effective enough.

But then we got a, 'Twin Tub.' One side spun round to wash the clothes which were transferred to the spin side to rinse and spin the water out. It stood in a corner during the week and had to be pulled out once or twice a week to the middle of the kitchen, for the washdays since there were very few socket outlets back in those days. It took centre stage a couple of times per week because of the volume of laundry from such a large family. It danced around the kitchen from the vibration and had to be repositioned frequently. You couldn't leave that baby alone for one minute or it could have ended up at one of the neighbours' houses. And the noise was deafening. All conversation was suspended while the twin tub was on and doing its thing. Then everything had to be hung out to dry on the close-line. No such thing back then as a clothes dryer. Whoever invented the dryer, to my mind, was practically the saviour of womankind, especially to mothers working outside the home. Him or her and whoever developed reliable contraceptives.

On the up side, my brothers were good to me. As they grew older and got jobs, they taught me how to drive and brought me to the carnivals on Saturday nights. There was no such thing as Night-clubs back in those days. Alcohol was not a requirement for enjoyment, in my youth.

They filled my Christmas stocking with money every Christmas. I hung my Christmas stocking up mischievously every year. Because they were older than me and had jobs, they always made sure I had plenty of money because they knew I was replacing their mother in so many practical ways. She was unable to perform the necessary tasks a parent would. And it fell to me to fill that role.

I began to have a lot of friends at secondary school when my peers there, especially the boarders, discovered I had several good-looking brothers. And they were always on the lookout for dates. I became a type of postman for a time delivering notes from some boarder or other to one of the brothers.

That was fun.

I enjoyed being popular for a change now that my tormentor had left school.

It held some light relief because, simultaneously, my mother deteriorated slowly.

The grandmother, whom I mentioned earlier, had been dead several years and the relief of that was profound for us children and my parents too I suppose.

But the damage had been done to my mother.

(Some psychology needed here maybe!)

And then, to top it all off, there was that accident I described earlier, that sent us all in to a downward spiral for some time.

But you know life goes on.

My friend Tina got a good Leaving Cert. and went off to do nursing. I went back to school for some points because the accident interfered with my studies the first year I sat the Leaving Cert. exams.

I made friends with a girl called Molly.

She had had a crush on my now deceased brother, so we hung out and I talked and she listened.

Wish I knew where she is now. She was one of those people that moved into and out of my life but saved my life for me with her patience.

A good person.

I hope she's well.

Tina, Molly, good people.

I got accepted into Trinity, with my extra points.

Yes!

Went along on registration day and registered and promptly told my brother Nick, who had driven me to Dublin city that I wasn't going to take up my place.

Philosophy and Latin!

Did you ever hear the like?

What would a country bumpkin like myself be doing with Philosophy?

True, my favourite subject at school was Latin. But I don't think that would have got me far in the world in those days.

Besides my mother needed me.

Or I was too nervous to leave the ashes! That is, leave home.

The College was traditionally the reserve of Church of Ireland upper class. It was established by Queen Elizabeth, not the current one, the one that was around at the time of Shakespeare, so it was a denizen of a class above mine. I got some very condescending looks on the day of registration and not having the benefit of moral supporters, I was out of my depth, I would say. Now I wouldn't be so, but that was my perception of things back then.

And in addition to this a maiden aunt of mine had drummed into me that doing Journalism in The College of Journalism in Rathmines, a real desire of mine, was no good to me and insisted I do the interview for teacher training in a Training College in Dublin instead.

Maiden Aunts. Back in those days. I thought we had rid ourselves of the authoritarian grandmother-type person. No such luck as long as this maiden aunt was around.

Don't you just love them? She usurped my mother's parental rights at every turn.

They're more enlightened nowadays, Thank God!

Interview!

I'd never done one.

I have done many interviews since but I have never done one that was so peculiar.

The teacher training interview for me went something like this…

I was doing grand I believe. I played my Feadog (tin whistle in English) fairly ok. Very important, it seemed, for teaching children two and two makes four.

I did the 'comhra', pronounced 'ko raw', meaning Irish conversation.

No problem.

Sat the numeracy tests and so on, thinking I was getting along just fine.

Then as I sat across the table from the heavy hitters of the Irish educational establishments, for the interview part, a man flanked by two Sisters of the cloth, I'm nearly certain I asked myself the question, as a complete moron, 'What the hell am I doing here?'

At the interview…

Rev. Sr. Habit 1 asked about my school.

Rev. Sr. Habit 2 asked me about family and I was name dropping nicely. I talked about my lovely talented maiden aunt, who was a principal in a local National school.

Then somewhere through the interview Mr Suit asked me, 'Do you believe in Mr Right?'

Well, that certainly clinched it for me.

The place in Training College. A total country bumpkin like me up against all the experience and wisdom of that particular third level institution.

What would I know about Mr Right? I had enough trouble getting through life as 'Right' myself!

Now I think WTF? I was cowed, mostly, but I tried. Me (a cake birdeen, local slang for 'girl in from the country'), going one-on-one with the great and mighty. I almost feel, after forty-odd years, that I didn't do too bad a job after all. Hey, they are all probably dead by now.

(On a side note regarding that interview: Nobody knows what their closest or remotest acquaintances might be going through but I always 'figure in' the 'maybe' scenario in a person's life. The interviewers wouldn't have a clue as to who I was, what I was capable of, what my life was like. Was the whole issue about Mr Right?)

Which is why I was a fairly good teacher, which is why I had to leave the system which had no fool proof solution nor answers for the broken child and was and is dis-improving because of the recent silliness and financial cutbacks in education provision. Fast forward here.

I thought I was making progress and then, 'puff', gone was the H.S.C.L. provisions.

Home School Community Liaison that is. I was given this post of responsibility as part of my job description.

I was good at that. I felt that I was being useful.

Anyway, back to that interview and I could picture my maiden aunt cringing at the thought of what I was I capable of answering. As she waited for me outside.

I bumbled and mumbled my way through an answer.

I've never told anyone this before not even my controlling maiden aunt who was a teacher herself and felt that dropping her name at the interview might swing it for me, plus she had driven me to the interview to make sure I went in.

So much for training college.

Pheww!

I dodged that bullet nicely.

So! Too short to be a guard, too silly to be a teacher trainee, too late to apply to Rathmines to do journalism, can't be a D.J. and too tired of nursing already... With my mum and all that.

Mr Right? W.T.F. was he on about?

For some people it's fairly straightforward. Marry the girl or boy next door. Childhood sweethearts. Live till a ripe old age. It's entirely possible. I know. Two of mine have done it. Many of my close friends have.

But back then, I wasn't so sure of myself or answers to hard questions like that. I have, with hindsight, come to altogether different conclusion to that question.

Later I will share some thoughts on that.

So I settled for a college course nearer home, in Galway.

I wouldn't say I flew through First Arts.

More like I 'winged' it.

Then I had to tackle second year. In those days, you had to carry three subjects and so I had to carry the math (a teaching subject, and Classical Civilisation which I loved was not of much use to me, so I dropped that) and as a result, I came a cropper.

Well, that and not studying!

I had met the man I was to marry so I was plenty distracted.

Talk about tall, dark and handsome.

Check, check and very check.

My offspring reflect his physical beauty. And his sense of humour. Thank God.

I was working in a local bar to pay my way through college, he came in with some friends and positioned himself at the end of the bar. I looked over at him and thought, 'I'm going to marry that man!'

Fell for him, hook line and sinker.

How could I resist the magnetism?

I couldn't and didn't want to.

So after a few dates we gave in to all our desires and the next thing you know we're expecting.

(Needless to say the maiden aunt left me out of her will!)

I tried, after our baby came along, to go back and repeat second year but the odds were stacked against me, even though I had the most amazing sister-in-law looking after my daughter when she came along. First paper maths flummoxed me. Always did, because the foundation for the concepts were not solidly laid. I could blame the teacher but it would be unjustified. Second paper Maths I loved. I could praise the teacher, and I am, justifiably. You get that from time to time. Good teacher; poor teacher.

So I dropped out and focussed on my family. My decision and only mine.

Him, me and Cora.

He wasn't too bothered if I dropped out or not so it didn't bother me. But I know my parents and brothers were none too pleased. As the only girl in the family with a good Leaving Cert they were probably hoping I'd be third level educated. So I was the one on this occasion directly responsible for the disappointment felt by all. Had Morgan been around he probably would have me stockpiling condoms, wherever he would have sourced them back in those days. Knowing him though he would have no problem.

He'd probably have clipped me round the ear as well for my irresponsibility. Oh well it's like I said earlier, he left a void.

Chapter 3

Then I had four children in quick succession in my early twenties.

Most people frowned on my prolific breeding. Or at least I thought they did.

I, however, wanted a mixed family but didn't want to spend years waiting.

Boom, Boom, Boom, Boom.

Done and dusted in a short period of time. No point hanging about.

My last outing to the labour ward added a brother to his three sisters.

Thank God!

I had nearly given up hope. But I knew I would have four. All my life before then, I knew I would have four children when I married. A mixed family!

They made me into the woman I am today.

Life in my twenties was a constant round of bottle feeding and nappy changing for about six years. Cloth nappies at that. No such thing as disposable, so the soiled and wet nappy had to be soaked first in Napisan or boil washed in a special pot. Needless to say the pot I had was immense and heavy to carry. Plus I didn't have the luxury of a washing machine for the first couple of years. Rental properties were only obliged to provide a fridge and a cooker. I did most of my washing at night when the children were asleep. It passed the time and bear in mind I was good at household chores.

I stuck fairly close to home twenty-four-seven.

When all my single friends were out and about and travelling!

I didn't care. I wasn't envious.

It didn't occur to me to care or be envious of them. I'm so glad I wasn't. Obviously naïveté and busyness occupied my mind.

I had a job to do.

Sitting on the floor when the children were little, playing with them and reading them stories. Having a routine.

Gathered round the dining table each evening doing homework, as they grew up.

Trips to and from school. I was practically living in my car at one stage, ferrying them back and forth to school from school, to various activities and sports and later part-time jobs.

I was 'it', when their dad was no longer around. The only person they had, to do it all.

I was the only person there was to look after them.

So I did.

It wasn't always easy.

It was demanding, tiring, challenging, lonely, and expensive. And I have to say here, not out of bitterness but to be real; I was not really looked after, financially, by the state back then. Not nearly as well as single parents are nowadays.

Which leads to a lot of my, later in life, cynicism towards 'the system.'

But I got through it for them and I was happy to. They will probably say I moaned my way through their childhood but for the most part I think I was nearly always totally financially challenged.

Whew, I'm glad that's over!

That wouldn't be the case today.

But, then, after I started working, I paid my dues like every other citizen. I feel I didn't get value for money then either, while the incoming populace did. They got looked after better than the indigents.

Me and thousands of citizens. But I did say I am not bitter.

We got where we wanted to get as a family not beholden to anyone or institution or government. It broke me financially to have to bear the whole burden but I have some satisfaction in saying we did it by ourselves and we owe nothing to anybody.

My children have grown up now and are all healthy and employed. What more could a mother ask for? They are also happy, well educated, polite, giving, funny, and conscientious. The list is endless. This is more than any parent can hope for.

Fair play to them and they are also best friends with each other. Still.

I lapsed into a depression in my late twenties.

It was probably dogging me for years. Ever since Morgan died. It was lurking around the edges of my subconscious. I was never unhappy you understand. But with hindsight I was probably a candidate for the blues.

Depression is a terrible thing. But you can come through it.

There's all sorts of help; the Samaritans, medical care, a little help from your friends.

Me?

Having tried all of the above…

I turned to a religious prayer group.

To fill the void.

It became very staged, so eventually, I bowed out!

After so many deaths, close personal ones, and so much religion coming at me from all sides, I have now finally arrived at the safe place of very simple faith.

Can't help myself!

Once bitten twice shy. Or is that twice bitten?

'Fool me once…' type of scenario.

That and being told by a member of the clergy who was preparing my daughter for First Holy Communion, 'The Virgin Mary in Heaven is your real mother.' I couldn't believe what I was hearing! And what did that make me? A uterus on earth? Who risked life and limb to give her life? Who sat up nights feeding her? Who hand washed her cloth nappies? Who administered the cold cloths to take down fevers?

Who worried sick when they, at different times, had to be taken to Casualty Department of the local hospital? Who took them to the local hospital? The Virgin Mary? I'm not castigating any religion but really, 'men of the cloth' should have got a grip on reality by now and I wasn't very impressed by what I was allowing my child to be told back then. Wouldn't that cause a conflict of identity? I'm sure the Virgin would agree, herself being a mother going through similar situations, with her own family.

That about sums up my disillusionment with 'The established church.'

So I dabbled, I suppose, in an alternative for a while until that bubble burst also. Being undermined is a terrible thing. Being led is grand until you find yourself relinquishing control to another entity. So I hate control and controlling people. I would never dream of controlling my children. My mother was undermined. She was controlled and I was by association controlled too. I relinquished control once too often.

I protect fiercely my own 'sense of self' and my family also have a great sense of identity as a result of making independent decisions. I do get very tempted sometimes to offer them advice but I have to stop myself and allow them to ask for it, whether they take it or not is their business. They are free people. As am I.

I'm not the smartest person I know but I think at this point in my life I'm probably one of the toughest people I know.

It's true. I am. I'd rather not be, by means of why I had to be.

I survived my first brother's death, although only minimally and, with a lot of help from my friends. As well as family.

What friends? My school friends, as it happens!

I never thought I had any, having been bullied for years.

'Tis a terrible thing to be bullied and in my subsequent years as teacher I was on a permanent quest to stamp it out. I even did a whole college course so I could help the struggling, marginalised, and bullied student.

Ego?

Well, maybe.

But I was fulfilled doing something altruistic.

After kicking the depression, I focussed on other people.

It's about when we look outside of ourselves and try to help others that we get all happy.

That's why I couldn't take my own life when I was twenty-six.

Too many of the aforementioned, *my* children, depending on me for their very existence. And thank God for them.

The reason I finally succumbed to depression was I had developed a crush on someone and I thought it was an unrequited 'crush'. It wasn't, as it happened, but I will explain that episode later. I went into a tailspin as a result of a misunderstanding between us and the depression that had been dogging at my heels for years, finally bit.

What does depression look like I hear you ask?

Well, getting out of bed is a struggle. Getting into bed is a struggle because you are afraid. Afraid of the expanse of night that you have to endure as a sleepless night. Fear and emotional simulations are your companions from night to dawn. Wide-awake-ness, when you should be winding down to sleepiness is what you experience and after several weeks of this feeling, you don't even want to bother going to bed.

Best scenario: you fall asleep around six am and wake again at eight am. Not drowsy awake but fully wide awake at four maybe even three. No rules. Fitful. One, two, maybe three if you're lucky, hours of sleep. Sometimes this only happens once a week. The rest of the time you are awake. Seventy-two hours or more. And you might get two hours of sleep. That's insomnia. On a large scale. And there's worse.

I know I have been blessed or lucky in my life but I often get asked the question. 'How did you survive all the tragedies?'

I don't know. I reckon I was born happy.

I know you might say, 'But you've been depressed'.

Ya.

But I'm still happy.

What can I say? It must be so.

Born happy. Look for a reason: you'll find a reason.

While I was married to husband number one…

(Sorry if I don't give 'them'; the husbands names, it may be easier for the reader if I give them numbers. And I'm not trying to be funny or flippant.

Just practical. As I've always had to be.)

So anyway.

As I was saying while I was married to husband number one, we saw more dinner times than dinners. That's because our family's limited resources were usually used on alcohol or gambling. Not my doing.

Now, I have serious issues with heavy drinking (especially drink driving) but they're nothing compared to the issues I have with gambling.

You can only drink so much money in a day and retire to bed through necessity i.e. passing out, but you can spend infinite amounts on gambling and not pass out and never get tired.

Every time I drive through any town in 'This Godly Country,' I marvel at the number of bookies or turf accountants or whatever names they give themselves to make themselves sound respectable, there are.

I think the country is held up, financially, by the revenue generated from said enterprises.

Must be so!

I should say 'bolstered' but maybe 'held up' is good irony! Or sarcasm!

They're mostly the only ones making money regularly in this country and you rarely see one 'going to the wall.'

They should carry a government health warning like cigarettes and alcohol and be renamed 'gambling establishments.'

And nowadays you can spend hours on-line gambling.

Bookies run in pairs with pubs. A quick way for spending all your money. Why does smoking and drinking get such negative exposure when gambling does not? I'm on a rant, I know.

Obviously, no one put the pack of cards or the love of 'the nags' in his hand or psyche, respectively. There is no one to blame. No one at fault.

I too like a flutter on The Grand National, love horses as animals and the odd game of snap!

But if you could judge a man successful by the number of friends he had in the bookies or the late night 'twenty-five' card game…He was popular.

Ordinarily he was such a hardworking individual though.

Stripped of his vices he would have been an excellent husband and father. He did the best he could, otherwise.

We did the best we could.

We were young and in love or in 'something'.

Well, anyway I have five live ones. Four from my first marriage. One from my second. As I said earlier, they're all working and they're all healthy. There is a God. But it has taken us all not a little while and a great deal of effort to get here.

Watching the movie Michael Collins, when Collins' aide told Kitty O Shea at the end of the film, 'he'd have no regrets Kitty'.

'But,' says Kitty, 'he would have said it better.'

Great line.

Love that.

No regrets.

It reminds me of myself. I have no regrets.

So when my first marriage got extinguished, I picked myself up dusted myself off and started all over again.

To live that is. It took a while. It was not easy.

But I got there and they got there with me.

We now call ourselves the 'boot strap family.'

Pulling yourself up by your boot straps on a regular basis will sear over any emotional callous that you have with enough practice.

With enough practice you can face any of life's challenges.

Children's illnesses.

Children's injuries.

Nights in E.R. by yourself. The others left at home with some kindly neighbour.

And I've had lots of those.

Kindly neighbours, that is, and nights in E.R.

Financial demands.

The list is endless. Most people would experience much of this in the everyday running of a home and raising a family.

I love my children. I also loved their fathers.

Some good news! After I remarried, I went back to college to get that degree which I had blown off several years earlier.

Husband number two was very supportive.

This didn't happen for me in my first marriage, as the man I had married at twenty, had more on his mind than college degrees. He wasn't against me going back to study after our baby came along; he just wasn't quite 'there' for me. I understand that as much today as I did then. That was fine then. It's fine now too. I too was a different person back in those days and at a different place emotionally and mentally.

Because, with him, I had knuckled down, and brought my lovely brood of chicks along. I realised my calling as a mother.

No more swooning over Roger.

The campus 'feek.' Local colloquialism for 'Ride.'

He wore his skinnies low, his zipper undone and cadged more lecture notes from his legion of fawning, female followers. Never having attended one himself, it makes me smile to see that he made doctorate and is now quite the authority on things historic. Our Roger has had a meteoric rise. On the backs of women. If only I were born a man. A good looking tall, semi, quasi, model type. With no possibility of becoming pregnant at the crucial time in life.

(As Juliet would say 'Aye me!'

But I'm no cynic.)

The perks of being a chirping, primping, fake type man, to get on in life.

At the right time and…maybe when you're with the right person, they bring out the best in you. I speak of husband number two here.

Jack.

Anyway, while married to him, I got my Honours Degree and managed through a random stroke of luck to get into the Higher Diploma in Education course.

What a pile of shite!

(I secretly wanted to do Communications. Well, not that secretly. I sussed it out and there were just too many obstacles to getting into that course. I would have too much travelling to do and be away from the family too long at a stretch at different times during the course. That's the second time in my life my plans as a journalist were scuppered. You'd think I'd get the message.)

So on to the Dip. Places were appointed on a 'lottery' basis back then. I had never won anything in my life before or since, so it must have been providence.

By the way, H. Dipping didn't prepare me for teaching at all!

Sorry former lecturers but cutting pieces of coloured plastic into shapes was utterly redundant in my teaching career. Showing up in front of thirty, or so, hormonally charged teenagers with different agendas to my own who wouldn't be too impressed with coloured plastic shapes should have spoken for itself even in the corridors of power in the college I so tiredly and grudgingly submitted myself for training for a year.

And paid well for it financially and otherwise.

Any libido I had in me was tortured out of me for a solid ten months while doing the revered Dip. And then I could live again. Until another tragedy stealthily sneaked its way into my life. More anon.

Anyway, I got an honour in the Diploma in Teaching as well as the degree. I must have a brain after all!

Not just a baby mill!

Then I was a teacher. I actually enjoyed the profession once I got into it. For several years I was happy to go out to work.

Loved Mondays. What were the Boomtown Rats on about? And Blondie?

I couldn't wait for September to roll around.

The new timetable and all that went with it infused me with life.

Seriously, it was a thrill a minute.

It was only a matter of time before someone or something rained on my parade.

I sound a bit fatalist but I'm not.

I'm a realist.

But enough of that for now.

Chapter 4

When I got together with husband number two, Jack, what a challenge that was?

To everyone, except myself it seemed, because he was older than me, and he was twice divorced. As well as that he was American.

And he was an alcoholic, in recovery. All the time we were together he never 'fell off the wagon' or had a 'slip' as they say in 'the programme.'

He worked in the Middle East when I met him first and he had a grown-up family back in the States.

Coincidentally, he was the oldest brother of my first husband, Gerry.

And no! There was no comparison between them.

Jack grew up in the States and for eighteen years he did not return home, so any similarities between him and his natural family had dissipated. That's why I found no resemblances there to his siblings and that's why I had no problem loving him having been with his brother. It was instantaneous. But not in that way. Not to begin with. I am very fond of my family-in-law. They have stuck with me through thick and thin. They understand me. I hope.

From the first moment we met we knew we were fated to be great friends.

Jack and I.

What was it about him?

Well, it was the way he actually got me. He understood me. Not that there was much to understand at that point in time after I first met him. I was fairly one dimensional.

All work. All babies. All housekeeping.

He hugged better than anyone else though. A hug that could say so much. Without words. And when I knew, that, in the circle of his arms, I was completely safe.

I had an ally, and that was novel. For me.

No need for words. It was silently understood. And when he stood in my kitchen and washed the spuds for dinner and peeled them, it was…

Oh! So comfortable.

His brother Gerry was usually out at work and I was left to my own devices. Make the dinner and do the laundry and feed the family.

I could have been having an affair!

I could!

Not that the thought actually occurred to me. I wouldn't know how to have an affair for one thing and I wasn't about to cheat on my husband. Jack would never countenance or suggest such a thing because he simply liked me and I simply liked him. Even in the early years back then, he wanted to mind me and protect me and that included my reputation and my marriage. It's not as if we ever discussed these things but I could sense it then and I'm sure of it now. He was my very good friend that flew in and out of our lives once in a while. I always felt I had space with him at every stage in whatever shape our relationship was taking at particular times in our lives together and not together.

With Gerry I had too much space. He was rarely at home but when he was, he had fun with the children and helped me cook and put them to bed. He was a dab hand with a bottle when they were infants, and always took them for drives when he had free time when they were little. But for the most part I did most of the raising of our children by myself. Physically, his departing didn't leave a big chasm in my life or the children's. I was used to coping by myself. Emotionally, I was heartbroken but I managed that recovery too after a time.

You may have sensed by now that Gerry died young and left me with a young family. I will explain later.

I know. I know. Everything will be explained later but I am in a hurry to get the running order of my life's main events down quickly.

And right now I need to explain about Jack.

Jack's life's story is unique. At least I think it is, but who knows? I could be wrong. But our life story together is unique as far as I am concerned.

His life is a lovely romantic odyssey filled with tears and anguish and anger and resentment and challenges. His story is happy but very sad. He was born in Ireland not far from where I was born. The same parish actually and just to set the record straight he was twenty-two years my senior. Not that the age gap made any difference to either one of us. But he said once that by the laws of average he would be gone before I would. I put that thought out of my head quickly enough, as you would.

He left for America when he was nine years old. He was accompanied by his seven-year-old brother. He wouldn't see his family again for nine more years. In the case of his brother it would be much longer. They swore allegiance to the American flag at the age of fifteen and became American citizens.

It was a cruel, but apparently necessary, 'deportation.'

Money was tight. Land was at a premium in the forties in Ireland. Making a living off the land was generally hard as holdings were small, especially in the West of Ireland, a throwback to the famine which was preceded for decades by the practice of subdivision of land. The parent divided his tenancy holding among his children. Thus making farms smaller and smaller as time went on and by the time the years of the potato blights hit, food was catastrophically in short supply. There was no fall-back supply of meat or grain crops, which were in plentiful supply especially outside of the West of Ireland but were exported, as per usual to the markets in England. Landlords' income you understand. Tenants, dying from starvation, be damned.

Ergo Famine.

In the 'forties', in the case of Jack and his brother Sam, cash was hinted at but never admitted to when the boys were fostered and I can't vouch for certain that there was anything more than a straightforward fostering agreement out of necessity. It was common in those days in cases of penury or ill health of a parent that a child be sent, temporarily to a relative in a nearby parish or county to be raised, but I'm not too sure if they went abroad. I only know that Jack and his little brother did.

They were given to be raised to maiden aunts. For the survival of all.

Well, the family survived.

The brothers were very affected by their parents' decision to send them so far away and who could blame them?

Even though they were well educated, and well provided for by their foster parents. No one could deny that.

They were sent to two different boarding schools in New York. They were literally separated at the point of entry at Ellis Island. Jack was to live with Maisie, the lady that collected them back in Shanbally in Ireland, Sam was delivered into the charge of aunt Maudie, who had never seen the child but waited for his delivery at the harbour.

'Pig in a poke,' you might say.

Sam had never met his aunts before a couple of weeks earlier in the case of Maisie and never before in the case of Maudie, his foster parent to be, and was inconsolable to not have his mammy and daddy there with him. Jack was the closest thing to family he would have in New York for years to come.

Seven is a very tender age.

They were college educated, and did very well by all accounts. Then they joined the armed forces, and like thousands of other Americans served their country faithfully.

But never again could they fit back in to their biological family as distance, time and a couple of maiden aunts put that possibility well beyond their reach for good.

Later in life Jack worked in Saudi Arabia. Whenever he was travelling to or from the Middle East en route to America or back, he touched down in Ireland to visit his family. In his forties he made one such visit. It was then I first met him. I was engaged to be married to his brother Gerry when I was in my twenties. The two brothers got on well and were close friends even though they had never met until a few years earlier. They were good drinking buddies. Jack was a fun-loving guy. He was also divorced when I met him first time.

About him!

What to say?

He was nine when he was packed off to New York.

They were going to send the second child but he was unwell at the time and too ill to make the trip. Talk about being lucky or unlucky or however you want to see it.

Anyway the aunt who adopted them at the point of selection, back in Ireland, Maisie, preferred Jack. He was more amicable. Not as surly as the second son. The seven-year-old, Sam, was intended for the other maiden aunt, Maudie, who wasn't so fussy and didn't attend the proceedings back in Ireland. She just waited for the delivery of her charge back in New York.

They didn't fly. The aunt didn't like flying so she booked a berth on a ship sailing out from Cobh to the new world, as many thousands did each year.

Common practice at the time. Emigration.

(It has come back in vogue again as the modern recession has hit.

The Irish solution to unemployment and destitution down through the ages.

Thanks largely but not completely, to an oppressive regime of 'Overlordship' and its subsequent legacy. Rule Brittania.

Although modern times have no one to blame but Irish politicians and bankers and greedy continental bondholders.

Talk about history repeating itself.

We relinquished sovereignty as we welcomed the policy of primogeniture from Henry 11.

Remember?

Better than election outside the clan!

Before that we invited help from the only British pope, Nicholas Brakespeare or Adrian IV as was his title, for help internally during the power struggle between rightful rulers in Leinster and Diarmaid Mac Morrough. Along came Strongbow, Richard de Claire. And the rest is history.

I suppose Adrian secretly or overtly wanted to bring the Irish Bishops, fairly autonomous individuals and lavished, financially, by the local chieftain, under the control of Rome.

More tithes for Rome, less financial shenanigans between the Bishops and Chieftains!

Then it was some E.U. Treaty or other, which dropped borders within the E.U. and Ireland of a hundred thousand welcomes, was born for sure.

Now it's the continental bondholders!

Some things never change.

Next it will be fracking companies.

Or China.

Or some Aga Khan or oil rich, spoiled, Sheikh or other.

At least only a *small* number of not very well documented and forgotten Irish ended up as slaves in the very unsavoury West Indies sugar plantations. Again I am being, morbidly sarcastic.

Nothing near the millions of less fortunate Black Africans, or should that be Negroid Africans which were shipped like cattle, and worse, from Africa year after year for centuries to satisfy the need for free labour in the plantations of the 'Southron' States of North America and the infamously barbaric conditions of the West Indies.

As Irish we do like our Reggae and Jamaican Irish.

The Irish deportees were mostly widows, orphans and priests. Got there by no choice. The West Indies, I mean. What we call nowadays Ethnic Cleansing!

Cromwellian solution to unwanted Irish riff raff.

But I digress as they say. My mind wanders sometimes. I am an historian at heart but also by profession. Quick history lesson there. Hopefully it's accurate.)

So the brothers got off the boat after five days of seasickness.

Jack and Sam.

Can you imagine how frightening it must have been for two young lads from the West of Ireland, aged nine and seven, being handed into the charge of women they had never met before, getting off a ship at Ellis Island to be confronted by the skyscrapers and the hustle and bustle of the city of New York.

Jack recalled the conversation his parents had had the night before he left.

He never understood why it was that they presumed he was asleep when they came to bed and had their conversations and such. Both himself and Eamonn, his younger brother, shared a room with their parents which was divided only by a makeshift partition. He didn't know if Eamonn ever heard their doings at night but he was aware of their couplings from an early age and listened in as they had their late-night whisperings and hushed arguments.

'Dan. Do you think this is such a good idea? After all he is our eldest son. Can't we send one of the others instead?' His mother pleaded.

'No Nora the agreement was we would send Jack. He is her favourite and besides Eamonn isn't well enough to go.'

'Feck her and her money. Thinks she can buy the world.'

'But we need it so badly Nora. Think of the other children. 'Tis hard to find the means to keep this family fed, and anyway he will do much better in the States. Besides he will be home here every summer like she promised or oftener if he needs to be'. Dan was becoming impatient with Nora.

'We should have kept to ourselves a lot longer between having babies. If you had kept to yourself a lot longer…'

'Don't be talking like that woman. After all a man has his rights when he has a wife. What would the priest say if he heard you talking like that?' He was becoming irate now. So was she. As usual.

'Feck you and your rights. Feck the priest and feck the whole feckin' lot of the whole race of man.' Nora was trying not to use curse words. She had long since dispensed with reverence for the clergy and she scorned the rights of man. Still, she was subservient. The law upheld the male prerogative, sex was his right and a woman had to submit to her husband's desires. And the church held the same view of marriage. Upheld the male prerogative. Women were goods and chattel.

'Mind would Nan hear you talking like that. You know how close she is to Father O Moore?'

'Feck her too, the meddlin' auld bitch. Sure I can't do a thing here unbeknownst to her. Can't bring up my children the way I want to. Can't turn nor twist without her leave. Sorry the day I crossed this threshold, what with you and your mother here challenging' me at every turn and now this, the child I spent two long days painin' over to bring into the world about to be sent away from me.'

'Hush you complainin' woman. Don't you think it doesn't upset me at all. My son and heir…'

Dan held his breath, not willing to upset his heavily pregnant wife. She was struggling with this pregnancy unlike the ones she had already been through. And of course there was a lot of truth in what she said. But right now they both needed sleep.

'Try not to worry Nora. Try not to worry.' Words as much for himself as for her.

'I'll try Dan,' she said as she rolled over and tried to sleep, in spite of the tremendous weight the baby was placing on her whole mid-section.

Jack drifted off to sleep then. There was none of the doings in his parent's bed anymore, since she discovered she was pregnant. He wished he didn't have to hear that. His mother nearly always objected. His father nearly always insisted. If Eamonn heard they never talked of it. Just pretended it wasn't happening or that the conversations were not overheard.

He woke to the sounds of Nan taking out the ashes to build the fire. Every morning since he could remember Nan started the day with the making of the open fire and before long she had the dough in the skillet to bake the bread for the breakfast. They had more in their larder than usual these days. Maisie had been generous with her money and they could enjoy some jam with their bread as well as an egg.

The other children who shared the bedroom with Nan were soon awake too and Maisie, who opted to use the settle bed in Nan's room, appeared shortly thereafter. His mother and father had gone outside to milk the cows and let the poultry out of their coops. It was usually Jack's job to collect the eggs but he was excused this day because of the day that was in it. Sam sulked all morning. They had been told they were going on a great adventure on a big ship to a city where Dan's sisters lived. It would be like a long holiday they were told.

Neither child knew what a holiday was.

Dan and Nora paced themselves for the rest of the morning. They were thinking of life without Jack and Sam. Thinking of Eamonn without his brothers each without the others, going without, coming without, always without, always so hard.

In the afternoon they dressed for the six-hour car trip that would take them to Cobh Harbour. The boys, along with their aunt, had berths on a ship docking at Cobh that evening to accommodate the many Irish emigrants heading for the new world. All hoping to make better lives for themselves as Aunt Maisie had done a quarter of a century earlier with her younger sister, Maudie. They were also helped financially to travel there by family members who had headed off to the States years before. A cycle that had been on-going for years, from Europe and Ireland in particular.

So they had hired the local hackney man, Tommy Docherty, who helped to load the suitcases into the boot of his car. Docherty had made this journey numerous times with other emigrants from the area. He made a good living from it.

As they were getting into the car, Nan was standing at the front door surrounded by his three younger brothers and sister. They were crying, as was Sam beside him. Margaret, his sister, was crying loudest of all. She was the little mother, his own mother depended on so much for help with the little ones. Misplaced responsibility and at such a young age. She wasn't yet eight. It was common in large families. And probably still is.

He said a silent goodbye to the low roofed thatched cottage with its two windows and the customary half door.

Smoke billowed from the chimney while the smell of the pigsty reached his nostrils, both smells mingling to create that unmistakeable smell of poverty. The two lean sheepdogs fought over a bone in the cobbled yard and a cart stood idly at a gate leading into the back garden. The chickens he had gathered so often in the evenings pecked randomly at invisible food, probably slugs, which was their mainstay nowadays as the meal ration was running low.

Red geraniums grew abundantly from the two window boxes, the one frivolity which Nora insisted on. And besides they grew easily enough and required no tending as such. She was too busy with surviving and raising a family to be distracted by frivolities. Women worked as hard as men on the land and save for a brief time-out for delivering and feeding children were back at work almost straight away after the birth. The older grandparents or older girl siblings took care of the infant.

Door and windows were red in colour and needed a fresh coat of paint. The thatch needed redoing, but the masonry itself got a new coat of whitewash when it was learned that 'The Yank' was coming for a visit. She sent the money in advance. For her keep and for some house painting.

The thatched roof would be taken care of when the harvesting and threshing of the oats was done. A back breaking dusty job that was done by a specialist called a 'thatcher'. A thatcher was an expensive spend, but necessary to keep the rain out of homes. He got well paid and was usually kept very busy but needed helpers from the home he was thatching and the straw from the year's oats was used on the dwelling house and sheds if there were any.

Jack waved to his younger siblings from the back of the car. They look puzzled and anxious and frightened. They had never seen their mother get into a car before, and in between sobs they shouted, 'hurry back mammy. Hurry back Jack. Hurry back Sam. Don't be long daddy.'

Nora resented leaving the children with Nan, but she had to see her sons off at Cobh. The two women rarely spoke except in tones of aggression or resentment. Nora claimed to Dan that Nan was trying to turn her own children against her. Prior to being married, her own mother had warned her about Nan, but Nora was easily smitten by Dan.

He was the best-looking man for miles around. He had coal black hair and was head and shoulders above his peers and when he would line out for the local Shanbally hurling team her heart would skip a beat. Single men and women enjoyed some free time at the Gaelic matches or the crossroads dances, their only outlets and social activity.

Then one evening at a crossroads dance outside the local parish church he turned her way and winked at her. She herself was quite a prize. Red curling hair which reached to her waist. She had the greenest eyes anywhere to be found. She was all woman and one could tell that having children would be no bother to her. That in itself was a prize to be coveted back in those days as having an heir to land was all important. Another throwback to the famine days.

He had 'set his cap' on her alright. The next thing she knew he was leading her to the dancing space. It was jig or a reel because in those days close dancing was not permitted and Fr. O Moore took his responsibilities seriously and kept a close eye on his flock. As the dancing came to an end for the night each went their own separate ways and as it was not the custom for married people to participate at the crossroads dances so all the single people were watched to make sure they left without a partner.

That night Dan had asked Nora to walk out with him which was as good in those days as getting engaged. He said he would ask old man Kelly to be their chaperone on the few meetings they would be allowed before marriage. They couldn't be alone together until their wedding night. She didn't hesitate.

The passion she felt for him that night had dissipated somewhere between the first child and the sixth. As foreplay was considered sinful, they tried to observe the rules of the church and mated solely to procreate children, a duty Nora could have done without as time wore on in their marriage. Dan, of course, enforced his male rights. That's the way it was. So she had no choice in the matter. Plenty of children, with none of the passion.

In the back seat of Docherty's car Jack was squashed beside Sam, while Maisie and Nora sat by the doors and neither one spoke very much as they were not blood related and neither one had set eyes on the other before this visit. Her children, Nora thought were being delivered to practical strangers.

'Feck her and her money,' Nora though, with a hint of jealousy.

Maisie was looking well on her fine living, while suffering none of the excesses of alcohol or poverty or childbearing. A childless maiden aunt, willing to take on the rearing of Jack.

'*He was by far the nicest of the children*,' Maisie thought, '*biddable and quiet.*'

He was also the eldest so he would require no molly coddling at all. Sam was another story.'

She wondered how it would work out for Maudie and him. She figured her sister might be sending Sam home sooner rather than later.

She looked around the lush Irish countryside and vowed she would never set foot in the place again. Too much narrow mindedness and religion. No thanks. She could well do without it. Scenery didn't do it for her. She was frigid and unromantic and had no time for such stuff.

'Scenery be damned!' It didn't pay the bills. She liked the anonymity of the big city where she could come and go as she pleased, not like Nora who was bound by so many rules and constrictions that living in a small religiously strangled community in the West of Ireland brought with it and no joy to any life or relationship.

'No! Good luck to that,' she thought. Internally blessing God and thanking him for the hand that life dealt her. Well, she had some religion still left in her. But at her own discretion and not from dogmatic manmade rules.

'There was Nora now, an old woman already from all that childbearing, teeth going rotten, veinous legs, no nylon stockings, dirt under her fingernails and probably hasn't had a hairdo since the day she got married almost ten years ago.'

She didn't judge her sister-in-law, merely felt pity and compassion for her. She made a mental note to send her the odd letter with money and a photo of Jack.

Later that day she led them up the gangplank and as the ship sailed out of Cobh harbour the boys looked back to take one last look at their parents before departing for their new home in a new country. It was very quiet and subdued on the dockside. Many of the departing emigrants were crying silently knowing they might never see their loved ones or homeland again.

Jack remembered all his life the pretty whitewashed houses of Cobh saying goodbye to him.

They were a stark contrast to what he was now going to be confronted with in New York.

To welcome him there, there were wide streets, lots of noise and traffic. The hustle and bustle of the big city.

Having said goodbye to Sam and the stranger he knew now as Aunt Maudie at the port, he embarked on one of his most terrifying and lonely journeys.

Multi-storey buildings mostly made from glass, sped past as they came closer to what would be his home for some time. The taxi ride from the harbour was so much quicker than the leisurely pace of the drive to Cobh Harbour with Tommy Docherty.

They were met at the front entrance of her apartment by a black porter called Willard.

She introduced the two of them, but Jack, who had never seen a black man before except in the geography books back home in Shanbally, was gobsmacked.

Being the friendly type, all six foot six of Willard bent down to shake Jack's hand.

What's a young lad to do in these circumstances, after suffering a sea voyage of several days, but empty the contents of his stomach all over Willard's highly shone shoes?

She was mortified.

She ushered Jack quickly into the elevator with as much haste as possible.

An elevator!

They dropped their few possessions in the lobby of the two-bedroom apartment.

Lobby.

What a strange new language.

Sidewalk, apartment, porter, lobby.

He was lost.

All alone.

He started to cry.

'Hush your wailin' now boy.'

She assured him, 'he was here for the better and that she would take care of him and that she would turn him into a fine gentleman and that maybe if he studied hard at school, someday he might grow up to be the president of America.'

As she cleaned him up, she considered again why she had done this.

She was on her own in the world since a number of years previously her philandering husband of two months had died in a car wreck as he drove his secretary home after some late-night work at the office.

She had had enough then of relationships and considered that she was as well to steer clear of them. She would have been a good catch too. She was tall and strikingly beautiful and advancing middle age only improved her looks.

Her late husband had left her quite an amount of money and even had taught her how to make her money work through stocks and shares and such.

Nevertheless she kept her job in one of New York's finest hospitals. Her job was everything to her. Made her independent and with it came a social outlet which she could have as much or as little of as it pleased herself.

At work one evening she saw an elderly lady die in the night with no-one there to see her off.

Maisie didn't relish the thought of that happening to her so she jumped at the chance to help her brother out with some money and in return she would foster Jack. Sam was meant to keep company with Jack albeit from a distance across town. New York is a big city. Across town was a long way off, logistically and time-wise and both women worked, so their meeting up was neither very regular nor desired. They led separate lives not out of dislike for each other but out of habit. But at least the two boys would be on the same side of the Atlantic. Which was consolation enough for Maisie and Maudie with respect to their nephews and charges. Hardly of much use to Jack and Sam.

Of course, across town, Sam was experiencing similar woes as his brother Jack.

His is another story. But I can't tell it.

Jack gave me his story as a present. It's mine to do with as I please he always told me as if he always knew I would tell it in print. That man sure knew me well. I was lost without him and still am. No not a father figure at all. Love of my life actually, truth be told. I bet Morgan would have liked him too, had they both lived.

Maisie, being the practical woman that she was she took him shopping the very next day, after they arrived in the States.

She bought him every piece of clothing, by three, and a suitcase. He had one already.

His parents had kitted him out as best they could in Geraghty's, the local drapers before leaving Ireland. They probably got things on 'tick' even though she had released money to them for expenses. The suitcases the boys had were old relics of times past, no doubt rounded up from benevolent neighbours when they heard of the upcoming travels of the 'young lads.' But she deemed it necessary for a gentleman such as himself to have plenty of clothes and cases to transport them in especially since he was going to go to boarding school.

She actually had to explain to him the concept of boarding school. She wondered if he knew anything at all about life. Little did she know he knew more than he would have liked to, having shared a room with his parents for so long. He became even more subdued when he realised she was sending him away to school. To be with strangers, in a strange environment, in a strange land with his strange aunt. He felt the isolation acutely but held back his tears. It seemed he wasn't supposed to cry. And so he internalised all those things, and all other setbacks thereafter.

She had his hair cut too, so that it wouldn't droop down over his eyes. She had it styled in the look of the day. Short back and sides and slicked back.

When he was suited and booted and groomed sufficiently, she looked on him proudly as if he had been her own creation.

And the following Monday he was promptly dispatched to a boarding school. The finest in New York city.

What business or experience had a middle-aged woman such as herself of raising children?

So she let one of the most illustrious schools in New York do that for her.

Why did she, a single nurse matron, adopt him in the first place she wondered many times?

Respectability. Mostly.

Having someone to leave all her money to when she died.

If sentiment came into the arrangement at all she kept it well hidden from him. So he grew up mainly loveless in a strange land without his family, and for the most part, without his little brother Sam. Life was far from happy back home, but he would have given anything to be back in his thatched cottage in the West of Ireland with his family and especially Eamonn, who, as well as being a brother was also his best friend. They did everything together, snaring rabbits, fishing with makeshift rods, learning to swim together in the local lake whenever time permitted outside of the chores they had to perform daily to earn their keep.

Because Maudie, the other aunt, lived a quiet life, as did she, they only met up a couple of times a year but as the boys grew up, they got together without the presence of their aunts and compared notes on school, women and other such important stuff.

Jack was the typical big brother and Sam needed him. Down through the hard years of New York they met as often as they could and talked about everything. Sam drew the line on conversation of Ireland as if he had a mental block about the land of his birth. That topic was not to be discussed and Sam would back away at any hint of Ireland, so eventually Jack stopped mentioning home and Eamonn and their family. Such was the hurt the younger brother was experiencing that he put up a mental wall concerning all thoughts of home. And his natural family.

As Jack stepped out of the taxi that first Monday morning at his new school several pairs of eyes were on him. He didn't notice at first but as he made his way to the principal's office, led by his aunt who had taken the morning off from work to settle him in, he felt as if he were under a microscope.

Jack who had to ask his aunt the Friday before what a boarding school was, felt a little nervous then. He knew he would be sleeping nights in the school he was to attend.

She knocked on Principal Sweetman's door and was ushered inside by his secretary where they filled out the necessary forms and were informed of the immediate details of enrolment.

Jack was permitted to go home every second weekend to stay with his aunt for the foreseeable future owing to the circumstances in which he found himself domiciled. Usually students were not allowed home in term time and it was hoped that Jack would settle in sufficiently well soon enough to stay the full term without home breaks.

She agreed to the terms of enrolment and satisfied herself that Jack would be looked after with special care for the foreseeable future. She was not about to cut him adrift totally and her attention to his malaise was a credit to her nature and noted silently by Jack and Mr Sweetman.

They set on him as soon as he left his unpacked suitcase on the bed. There were at least six of them, Jack noted. They knocked him to the floor and kicked him severely several times into the gut. Blows that could not be seen without him undressing.

'Don't get up you Mick, and don't go squealin' to nobody unless you wanna get more of the 'special treatment'. Trevor is countin' on your silence. You have too many enemies here to come at us. Just stay nice and you'll be fine,' one of the assailants sneered.

Sometime later he hauled himself off the floor and fell into his bed where he passed out from both fatigue and anger. He was nine don't forget.

The school week started for Jack on Tuesday and, still sore and reeling from the beating he had taken the night before, he queued up outside classrooms where he thought he was meant to be.

His last school in Shanbally had twenty children give or take. He figured this one had maybe five or six hundred students.

Several days later he found himself being rescued from the Duncan gang by the kindly Miss Gately. In the schoolyard. They were becoming more brazen.

Trevor Duncan and his cronies were established silver spoon American offspring of third generation settler.

Mr Sweetman and the staff decided to move Jack up a year because he was older than his present year group and had good results in entrance tests. He left the mob then for an advanced year. And Mrs Gately watched over him.

After several months of peace and quiet and being left alone, he saw another victim of the Duncan gang being harassed. He looked to be Italian or thereabouts. Jack walked up to Duncan and laid him out with a right hook that would have made Marciano proud. After that Jack befriended the Italian boy, whose name was Toni Fallini, a child of well to do owners of an Italian restaurant.

As Jack moved through the American education system, he resigned himself to the fact that she was not going to take him home on a visit anytime soon. At first he pleaded and begged her to let him go home. Home was out of the question she told him. She enforced the fact that New York was his home now and that she was his guardian. As the visits between himself and Sam were so infrequent, his friendship with Toni strengthened year on year. She allowed him to pay regular visits to the Fallini restaurant. While he was visiting there, he had the closest semblance to a family he had ever had and thereafter. The Fallini family were strict Catholics. That's why she accepted them, he supposed, and every Sunday he was home from boarding school whenever Toni was home, he attended Mass with them and hung out for the day. They all ate together at dinner time and Jack was always a welcome guest. As he grew older, he was allowed to have wine with dinner as was the Italian custom. Jack liked how the alcohol made him feel mellow and he did not feel the pangs of homesickness as much. He also started smoking, something she didn't object to as she felt that he was making independent decisions, so it was all the better. It was settling him somewhat to have close family ties with the Fallinis and so long as he was coming up with the grades at school, she was happy.

He was an above average student and that pleased her. At least her dream to have him well educated was coming to pass.

He was growing in stature and manners. He was refined and handsome and she was proud to introduce him to her friends as her 'son' a term he objected to but not vocally.

Sometimes she would take him to the cinema or to the theatre. Goodness knows there were enough of them in New

York. He enjoyed the productions and the operas. Toni went on occasion also. The family were keen Opera goers, something that was built into their Italian blood.

Toni had an older sister called Cassia and a younger sister called Maria.

Both were beauties but Jack fell silently and totally in love with Maria. As the time came to a close on the high school years of Jack and Toni, they had decisions to make. They would sit on the back stoop of the Fallini restaurant and dream of their futures. Jack would enjoy a quantity of alcohol on these occasions which would make Toni concerned but would say nothing.

They always ended their visits with a hug and a handshake and return to boarding school the following day and settle in to the next week of education.

They were best friends for years until the Vietnam War separated them. They both volunteered, and they signed up together.

Toni was blown to pieces by a land mine somewhere on the Ho Chi Minh trail as his platoon tramped through a mosquito ridden swamp.

He was twenty-two.

He had been in Vietnam one week.

Jack had avoided active service because he had a plate fitted in his leg back in Ireland, when he was a child, after a serious farm accident involving a cartwheel.

Another loss.

Toni.

And before that his family.

But he was really stung when Toni's sister Maria decided to get engaged to Robert Decaccia.

Jack had long held a passionate, secret desire to be Maria's man but he could never share his longings with anyone. He didn't know how.

Then, at the funeral of his best friend, he learned of the upcoming nuptials.

And yet another loss.

Loss was becoming a life issue for him and no doubt for his younger brother, whom he hadn't seen for six months.

Sam had enlisted into the navy and was discharged honourably when the cables which caught the planes as they landed on aircraft carriers severed three fingers of his right hand.

Sam did what he normally would do to ease the pain. He went on a bender and ended up in rehab in Hawaii several weeks later.

The navy was good to Sam and paid him a serviceman's pension for the rest of his life. Unlike Jack he had never returned to Ireland to visit his family. He had some years earlier changed his name to Sean Makenna and disowned the land of his birth and his parents whom he had thought abandoned him when he was going through his formative years.

Jack, however, had returned one time to see the family when he was eighteen. And he stuck out like a sore thumb.

His hair was different. His clothes were different. His accent was different. He wanted to help around the house, and with the dishes and that was a 'no-no.' That was women's work.

Two days after he arrived back to Ardmore not to Shanbally, where they all had moved after the two boys left, a much bigger holding, it was announced that the hay was going to be saved on the morrow.

'Farmers have such nice ways of saying things,' he thought.

Saving the hay.

Footing the turf.

Dagging the sheep.

Skulling the cattle.

The middle field.

The far field.

The top field.

The bottom field.

Over beyond!

He was in heaven.

He was very excited about the haymaking as that was what he remembered most from his youth.

He was challenged to remember all the names of his brothers and sisters because several children had been added to the family since his departure half a lifetime ago.

Some of them were babes in arms.

They had a family dinner the evening before. A hurried affair without much conversation. The males ate first. The women ate afterward, when the men folk were fed.

It was quite unlike the Fallini family dinners.

He was a regular guest at the Fallini table.

They were noisy, and yet sociable affairs. Everyone got to sit down together. Everyone allowed and expected to contribute to the conversation. There was much animation and loving gestures among the family. They usually shared a bottle of wine or two.

(The seeds of discontent sown in Jack's life several years earlier with his exile had not yet produced a crop, but would sprout sooner or later.

His downward spiral into alcoholism was slow but inevitable.)

However there was no alcohol at the table in Ireland. The father had a bottle of stout. That was it. Jack was a bit disappointed he wasn't offered a drink of some type. He was over age after all!

Next morning they were up at the crack of dawn. The weather was just right. The hay had been cut and was drying. Was turned and was ready for the tramping and saving. His father was in good form and rounded up the boys and they all headed off for the hayfields.

Jack couldn't understand why they were so unenthusiastic. He had forgotten that life on the land was hard and had he taken time to think back he would have remembered he was less than enthusiastic as well, as a youngster.

Now he was a holiday maker.

An onlooker. They were stuck with their lot on the land.

Their demeanour was sullen to a man and they grumbled along all morning until their father threatened them with being sent to live in Nan's house, in Shanbally, their former home, to take care of her. She lived on her own in the next village and was quite contrary.

None of the boys obviously relished this prospect and so they worked silently for the rest of the day.

The women joined them in the afternoon as all hands were required on the farm.

At least he could have a normal conversation with Eamonn. The second oldest and the one that Jack remembered most. Eamonn enjoyed some autonomy as the oldest remaining son from that day long ago, not Jack anymore, and the one who would inherit the farm. So Eamonn's motivation for work was different from the rest of the family. They were closed down. Silent. They didn't open up a conversation spontaneously. The father was the one to initiate conversation and they rarely joined in.

As Jack was a novice to the task at hand, he provided them with some private humour throughout the day.

He was beginning to think his life wasn't so bad after all.

They would all be sooner or later in competition with each other.

Over land.

Jack had his aunt's money to look forward to.

No competition.

They would be forever jostling with each other for favour with their father over this piece of land or that piece of bog.

If this seems like a digression, it is a necessary one to paint a picture of the early life of my beloved Jack. Of what shaped him. How he ticked. How he filtered life's situations through his abandoned self.

Back in the US, after that first trip home, Jack was busy making a career for himself in landscaping, his major in college. And then life as a serviceman in the air force. He had suffered through Toni's death, Maria's marriage, his aunt's untimely death.

And I was a baby.

Growing up in the West of Ireland.

Our paths met when I was engaged to his brother.

The fact that I was pregnant with my first baby hastened that auspicious occasion.

Marriage. Shotgun style.

It's not like nowadays where you don't have to be married at all or even thinking about it before having children.

Nowadays it's a career move for some!

No! Back in the seventies. It was disgraceful to be pregnant outside of wedlock. And women had no access to contraceptives of any kind in those days. Keep your legs crossed!

Not so much a disgrace for the man.

As if the sperm are airborne and ingested through the nostrils during that particularly fertile time at about twelve days after a period.

How unlucky can a girl get?

All those things operating in perfect union.

Result.

A pregnancy.

He doesn't count.

He did nothing.

The men were always off the hook. Cynical: I know.

Anyway as I tell my firstborn all the time, 'you made me.'

'Tis true, my life was spinning towards some parallel universe and then she came along and it all made sense.

I had focus.

I had purpose.

Didn't need manuals or anything.

I had a child.

Then two.

Then three.

Then four.

Yep.

They were accumulating rapidly and then I shouted stop.

Woah Nellie!

Feck this Billings method! I was too busy to stick red and green and other coloured stickers in a chart. And anyway I didn't have a cycle.

'Doc, give me the pill.'

I thought he would run me out of his surgery.

But I held firm.

We reasoned.

He relented.

Back in those days contraception was unheard of. Well, the use of was unheard of.

But I figured if the seed was practically airborne, I'd better take precautions!

You see we were fertile with a capital 'F.'

And then Gerry, husband number one was gone. Another road death.

One fateful night in April, he ran out of luck.

If he ever had much.

Those of us who do can shake our heads all we like.

He was always behind.

He waited always for that one win.

I sound somewhat cold.

Well, actually I was devastated.

I loved him. He loved me.

He loved his children.

He was a good guy.

He was funny, energetic, intelligent and deep.

Inherently sound.

But he had a problem.

You probably have picked up on that by now.

But there's no other way to state the facts.

Our baby boy was nineteen months.

So I picked myself up, dusted myself off and started life all over again.

Another loss.

That makes two. Three if you count the ailments of my mother.

Then again, I have lovely children.

Sudden death is a terrible thing.

Death from cancer or other terminal illness is a terrible thing.

For those left behind they are both bad things.

I can't make up my mind which is worse.

But the one who goes suddenly, is saved the agonies of dying.

The sick person has no such immediate release.

So for them we all know which is worse.

But for those left behind?

Well… you make up your own mind.

So there I was a widow at twenty-six.

It's not even a nice word.

Widow. I know I may have said that before.

Well, what happened was…

I was sitting at home, in our rented house, this particular night as I always did, knitting, when there was a knock at the door at about ten o clock or so and being one for security I considered not answering. I did have a dog and a late-night knock is a curiosity arouser. Besides I had a bad feeling. And I almost knew what it was about. Standing at my back door was a well-known and well-liked priest.

'Oh my God this can't be happening.'

But it was.

He didn't have to open his mouth to let me know that my husband was gone.

Following shortly on his heels were the brothers.

They packed me up lock, stock and barrel and took me back to my parents' house with my little sleepy brood, which were called out of their warm beds for the journey.

They were either just getting over the measles or getting them. My baby boy Finn was right in the middle of being sick and as a result of travelling and attending a funeral suffered a mini stroke and blindness in one eye. Partial sight in the other eye. They say you should keep measles sufferers in a dark room. Back then there was no M.M.R.

But I was too grief stricken to notice. They became the responsibility of the family for the duration of the funeral.

Another blur.

Another loss.

People are great when you need them.

It felt as if the funeral lasted weeks instead of days.

When would all this end?

Too many people.

All of them cared.

He was liked.

I was guilty. Guilty of what I don't know.

Guilty of being too busy with lots of children and that we had run out of time for each other.

But hey! He always knew where I was. I could only guess about his whereabouts.

Now he was eternally stationary.

The blossom in my hand was loosened by someone to drop it into his grave. I was too numb and too shocked myself to let go of it. The worst thing about funerals… watching a coffin drop into the ground and being buried by clay.

I'm grateful Jack opted for cremation.

We scattered his ashes in his favourite place on the planet.

Coran Lake, to the strains of:

'The answer my friend is blowin' in the wind.

The answer is blowin' in the wind.'

I didn't take Erin to this scattering of ashes ceremony.

I reckon she had been exposed to enough questionable activities. Her dad's sickness and such and I felt the older ones were immune to grief at that stage.

Hindsight proved they were not.

And years of counselling later attested to this.

Being a mother is not easy.

But you get better at it over time and weathering storms was becoming increasingly frequent and normal for me.

I hope I don't have to be a 'sage' grandmother.

What I mean is I hope they have it easier than I.

I hope all is well for the next generation.

Better than I had it.

Hopefully. So many 'hopes' there it's like a prayer, wouldn't you say?

It seems to be going well.

So after I had been moved back home by the brothers, I had to try to rebuild a life for myself and my babies.

And one afternoon about a week after I had buried my husband, Jack came by to visit. He had his 'wife' with him. Well, his soon-to-be-ex. But I didn't know that at the time.

He was gorgeous.

She was a bore.

What was he thinking of?

How could this very interesting man be with someone so one dimensional?

Or was I just being judgemental? Probably.

After all I never had a singular emotional feeling in my life and all of a sudden during the week when I had buried a husband, I was having a…A what…?

An emotional reaction!

I like this guy too much.

This particular week I shouldn't like anyone but I knew I'd liked him for forever.

And that I would love him for forever.

I was jealous of her. Simple as that.

Little did I know they were on their way to getting a divorce.

I was broken and bruised. How could I have feelings of any other kind?

But I did.

More guilt.

God.

Is there no end to the complications of the human heart?

Answer.

No.

Why am I so sure?

I'm sure. Life's experiences, God help me.

Sometime later, after Gerry had died, I was given a local authority house for me and my brood. It was pure heaven.

I did it up the way I wanted it and had just about enough room where I didn't have too much.

So I brightened up by the day. Bought myself a small car. Was very independent. Doing it all. Enjoying life.

The children were doing well in school. Finn was having his eyes corrected. Thank God that problem was coming right. A definite gain I would say.

And then after a year or so Jack came back into my life while he was on a flying visit to the states. Apparently, to finalise his third divorce. His second, from his present wife. To pay his lawyer and to get his Decree Nisi. We had kept in touch, albeit infrequently, by letter.

I don't know if my kids know this. I do not intentionally withhold information from them. I must share this fact with them soon, especially Erin, my child by Jack. She would probably find it interesting.

By the way this is the person that I had the misunderstanding with about feelings for each other, which led to my depressed state, which I have mentioned earlier, but as time went on, we sorted ourselves out and ultimately got married the following year.

We got married in a registry office in Wandsworth, in London.

It was the week before Christmas and I flew over to London with my friend Jane as a witness.

Why London you might ask?

He was not domiciled in the country at the time as he had taken a new job in Riyadh.

So London was our most convenient option.

No white wedding for me this time either. My last walk up the isle was at a not so local church to stay away from the local gossip. I had worn a suit and thankfully I didn't look pregnant on the day so the wedding photograph didn't reveal anything.

Jack had asked a friend of his in London, to be his witness and together with him and his wife and Jane, we all got into an old Morris Minor and headed to Wandsworth. I can't remember what I wore that time. Must have been some kind of low-key outfit then as well. I have to say it was made all the more special because Jack had commissioned a bespoke diamond ring for me in Riyadh. It was as original as he was and as special as we were together. We opted for Claddagh rings for wedding bands because he liked the idea of something uniquely Irish and I had already done the plain gold band thing with Gerry.

After the ceremony we had donuts for wedding cake.

We flew home to Ireland and the children the following day.

They were delighted to see Jack, who had been staying with us for a time before going back to Saudi four months earlier.

They were also a little miffed that they had not been a part of the nuptials.

They still jibe me about it, especially in front of other people. It's their way for being funny. They will always pull out the 'I was such a mistreated child' card in company!

'She didn't tell us she was getting married…' and on and on.

Way back then, when Gerry and I were together we didn't own our own house so we moved a lot. The children sometimes have this parlour game nowadays. Guess how many moves. I think I have made my final move, where I am now.

One move we made was to Riyadh.

Which is a book in itself. Or at least it merits a chapter.

Chapter 5

Prior to Morgan's death, I remember the summers were long and languorous. Not like any summers we've had since. Washed out affairs. Not up to much, or would that be psychological because of what happened to me?

You'll all remember those kinds of summers...If you're old enough, like me.

In those years of my childhood, the sun rose high in the sky each summer for weeks on end. May, June, July, August. The open countryside was a feast for the senses.

The days were always long and bright. There was a remarkable summer haze. The colour which only summers like those could produce. Summers were balmy, warm, mirage-like towards the end of the horizon. The faraway steeple and church were barely visible then because of the haze.

In the morning when the overnight fog of summer had been dissipated by the rising temperatures it was replaced by that beautiful, blue, heat haze.

And each night as the sun went down the gossamer producing fog would descend over the bog which lay between our house and the local town.

The bog smelled sweet and dry and musty and ancient. The rotted woods that had laid down the bogs thousands of years earlier smelled like a fine old port wine as I recall now.

When the trees died and decomposed, they produced an essence of calm and quiet, which is being recreated artificially in many health spas in modern times, and generating much revenue for five-star hotels.

For us, in our formative years, it was free and therapeutic.

The most tranquil place on earth.

Or was that childhood innocence?

Natures toil and decomposition and decay produced such life and such relaxation.

The shades of the bog varied between a rich chocolate brown and an alluring shade of purple.

The colours of the bog commingled with the blue incandescent haze of the atmosphere and produced a natural masterpiece with a mystical peace.

Butterflies hovered over the flowering heather, enthralled by the smell and the sights. Their lively wings beat out the tempo of temptation which the wildflowers provided. Orange and white and red. And yellow.

Butterfly silence settled over the bog. The crickets 'cricked' all day as if they were protesting the heat.

The bog-holes and turf reeks, purple heather and brown cutaway bog face all worked together in perfect harmony to produce a wondrous, picture-perfect summer scene of serenity.

The cows meandered softly along their time worn tracks aware of the dangers of venturing off the paths lest they become bogged down in muddy holes.

Somewhere in the distance, the braying of a donkey stallion could be heard and then the answering call of a jenny several miles away.

Swallows swooped, flitted, dived passed and were gone.

Evenings brought migratory birds flying in formation.

Silhouetted against the darker blue evening sky.

In the summertime our men folk saved the turf for the winter fires. Also known as peat to non-indigents, it was backbreaking work. They had to cut it with a slane, foot it, turn it, re-foot it, clamp it, stack it and eventually bring it home. As the only girl it fell to me to make bottles of tea and ham sandwiches and take it to the bog for the hungry men. I used to ride to the bog on a donkey called Elvis to deliver the much-anticipated refreshments. Well, back in the seventies what else is a girl with such a cute donkey for a pet going to call it?

Occasionally there was a bottle of Cidona and after distributing the food and drinks I took myself off back home to start readying the dinner or doing the washing.

Summer days were long, just six hours of darkness at the summer solstice but all too soon autumn and schooldays were inevitably approaching.

Then the weather would change. The rain would start to fall at the end of August. The hazy colours were dispersed by the grey drabness of showers. Lines of rain traced across the bog and the sky gradually closed in, changing shades from a brilliant azure of blue to grey and then to dark grey.

Sandy smells rose in the air replacing the clean dry smells of dust.

The once visible horizon would vanish and nearby villages would barely be discernible in the distance.

The rich browns and purples of bog vegetation would take on darker shades of each colour.

Summer was drawing to a close.

The temperatures didn't drop much straight away.

The music of washing and flowing water mingled with the smell of wet dust and green lushness.

The sounds of summer were replaced by the pattering of huge raindrops against the galvanised roofs of the sheds and the plink plonk of the rainwater overflowing the burgeoning eaves chutes into the barrels ready for collecting the pure water.

The barrels on either end of the barn would steadily fill up making the soothing mellow sound of liquid in wood.

Water seeped out between the dried-up laths of the barrels but they would swell and hold.

Animals would gather to the dry side of the stone walls and ditches or just stand with their rumps to the rain in the drenched fields.

Torrential then. Rain. Rain. Rain. The stuff of life.

Water flowed down the worn gullies on either side of the road washing away the dust and exposing the well-polished larger stones of road foundation.

Dry cow dung swam downhill in its path.

Water joined other rivulets from side roads, and filled the water tables to the brim.

The heavy moisture bent dog leaves and ferns downwards and drenched wildflowers and grasses till once stately growing things had to bow beneath the beating of the showers.

Hens and other farmyard fowl took refuge in old barns, under ripening fruit trees or flew up into the rafters of the hayloft and seem to suspend there as time stood still waiting for the deluge to pass.

The donkey and horses stood stately together and occasionally rippled their midriffs when horseflies attacked. Tails of cows and beasts alike swished to ward off the menacing midges that had multiplied in the heat and the humidity.

Breathing became sluggish.

The summer freshness was replaced by oppressive autumnal air.

Increasingly the sky lowered and farmers who had not completed the summer work cursed the much-needed rain and prayed it wouldn't last past a couple of hours.

We children knew the summer was drawing to a close.

It was the end of the carefree summer days. Schooldays were imminent.

After the accident I don't recall summers being so pleasant.

They all seemed to be grey. Rain, which was once a blessing, seems never to have let up since. That summer was an end to all summers for me.

By contrast, The Ar Rub Al Khali desert was the most beautiful place I had ever seen. Not that I had done much travelling in my life mind you but the feel of the heat, the hot sand between my toes and the smell of the dryness almost replicated the summers of long ago in Ireland.

The summers before the accident.

I went there with Jack and our children to live just after we had been married. I mention this now to draw comparisons and contrasts between Ireland and Saudi, if there are any. Well, I thought so.

Added to that the fact that I was with Jack, and we all, as a family, were enjoying life so much I somehow got back long forgotten feelings of freedom and which I enjoyed as a child.

My first impressions of the desert were I suppose the same as anyone else's would be.

The first night we arrived, it was mid-February. It felt warm. Little did I know that the temperatures would rise to over forty-five degrees in summertime. At fifty they stopped counting. In February it was about thirty or so. The evenings were cool, about twenty degrees.

In the days and weeks that followed we travelled mostly with Jack. We took trips in the evenings. The days were getting longer. The overwhelming colour was sandy brown. Obviously, since Riyadh is situated in the middle of Saudi, or near enough. And much of Saudi is sand. The predominant tree is palm. The main shrubs are low growing, mostly acacia and stubby cactus. Homes were built from a type of sand the colour of the desert although the desert sand was unsuitable. Apparently the sand to build the modern villas was imported. The older dwellings of the nomadic settlers would be constructed from local sand and blocks, in the form of mud mixes somewhat like wattle and daub building.

There was no pervading smell of sand save when the rainy season would come for about a week in February. Even then rain was sporadic. During the wet season I could smell the sand mixed with rain and was not unlike the smell of the distant summers of my past in the West of Ireland.

Mirages obviously are a phenomenon of the desert from the extreme heat and reminded me of the hazy blue heat over the bog in Ireland whenever the temperatures there climbed high enough to produce mirages.

In Riyadh there was very little wildlife visible. If one looked for wildlife, butterflies could be seen. Small lizards, known as salamanders, climbed the walls of the villas and took refuge from the heat in cracks in the plaster in the walls. Stray saluki dogs were a common sight as were mongrel cats. Very scruffy animals with a mean streak in them. Expats kept pets, but well out of sight from the rest of the world. For the safety of the animal, naturally. Anything was on the menu for the poorer third world expatriates.

Obviously, camels were a usual sight but you generally had to drive out of town or into the suburbs to see them. Most animals were generally the colour of the desert, although the nomadic herds of goats and sheep could be white, black and white and black.

A pleasant day out could take you to the zoo where the animals were well cared for. Exotic coloured birds were very plentiful and sometimes they could be on display in the public parks in practical bird friendly cages if there is such a thing.

The contrasts to the West of Ireland are enormous, and the comparisons are few but some-how I felt very much at home there.

Normally, whenever I am asked if I liked living in the desert, the answer is always the same.

'I loved it.'

I usually added that if I ever had the chance to go back I would, whether to recreate something which was nice and good, life with Jack or simply, I liked the desert.

I must mention for the record how Jack and I got together. After all we lived in two different worlds and two different continents.

One day about a year and a half after Gerry died, I had this letter out of the blue.

From Jack.

Ah! It was so romantic in a purely friendly sort of way and I, still being somewhat naïve, and in mourning, thought it was a very improper 'come on.' So I shoved it as far back into my secret drawer as I could. Actually I had to devise a secret drawer on the spot, never having had one before. Never needing one. What secrets did I have at my age and stage in life? But I was a bit panicked so I had to keep that a secret.

I took 'The Letter' out several times that day and read it again and again.

And for several days after.

If only I could, I thought.

I let my mind wander to places I never would before.

And doing things I never should before.

It was a pleasant aside from the daily trips to the school and the mundane washing and ironing and cooking.

He promised to visit me in the springtime.

I secretly looked forward to it. I always enjoyed seeing him.

But that was when I was married and didn't have any thoughts beyond the friendship of a family member. We wrote back and forth occasionally in those days, as husband number one saw fit.

What was it to me?

A letter from the brother-in-law.

Nothing more.

This was different though.

Then one day I saw sense.

I tore up his letter and wrote back to him.

I told him in no uncertain terms that we could never be lovers.

I also asked him to never write to me again. And not to visit either. I shut him down quite forcefully and effectively.

He took me at my word and I heard no more from him.

Little did I know that he was slowly going through his twelve-step programme and his sponsor suggested he do as I had requested.

So I waited and waited for a sign of some kind. Another letter would be good.

But it never came. And I watched out for him on the appointed day he was supposed to have visited in the springtime as planned.

He never came.

I was deflated. And I became more deflated by the day. I missed his friendship so much then. I was all mixed up. I had been sailing along nicely in life and then 'He' happened.

Honestly there should be rules to this game and I wasn't even used to playing it.

I grew more introverted by the day.

I was doing what I always had done, looked after the home and the children and yet the ordinary things were becoming alien to me.

I began to have disturbed nights' sleep. I woke earlier in the morning. I was getting restless. I was coping for the most part, but then the anxiety set in.

Then the panic attacks.

Then I could no longer make myself stay in any one spot for any length of time. I stopped going out with my friends. I was becoming more detached from reality by the day. I used to leave my shopping, unfinished, in the middle of the aisle at the supermarket. I used to feel nauseous for no apparent reason. Anywhere and everywhere 'the panic' could strike. I became fearful of attending events as a result. I was functioning less and less every day. I was hearing voices. I thought I had a late vocation. The Samaritans were called a few times.

I was suicidal.

The doctor once told me as I lay in, what I thought was, my sick bed as he did a house call to my house, that I needed to get up and get on with it. That I was alright. And as it was a fine sunny day, he opened the curtains in my 'sick room' and left, to let me 'get on with it.' That was his diagnosis.

Just like that. I was alright. Nothing wrong with me.

I have since come to recognise the symptoms of depression and yet this trained professional just thought I needed to 'get on with it.'

I had no issues with the man. So I tried to do as he suggested. But my feeble attempts at 'getting on with it' failed miserably.

So I did the only thing I could think of.

No.

Not tell my family.

Although I've a fair idea they knew something was wrong with me.

I was lack lustre on all levels. And behaving fairly morbidly.

No. I called Jack. He would know what to do.

After all, I was happy before he happened along, with his love letter and not showing up when he should and all that.

How dare he?

Didn't he know how much he had impacted on my life?

On my nice little existence.

With no pressure.

I rounded up as much fortitude as I possessed at that time. A bit like 'The Interview' I had done a lifetime ago, I felt as daunted then too.

I prayed and crossed my fingers and sat staring at the phone for ages before I plucked up enough courage to dial his number.

'Hello.'

His voice the other end of the phone was all I needed to hear.

'This is Cathy.'

'Well, hi there. I'm so glad you called.'

Him and his Yankee accent. And his cheerfulness. And I dying off.

'You are?'

'Sure I am.'

'Where were you? That time you were supposed to visit?'

'Well, you told me not to write or call you or see you so I took you at your word.'

'Well, I missed not seeing you.'

'And I missed not seeing you.'

'You did?'

'Of course I did. I love you.'

'What?'

'You heard me. I love you.'

With his twelve steppin' he must have been trippin'.

But just like that he said it and everything fell into place.

We talked for a while and made plans and laughed and chatted and caught up.

Then we hung up. It was my parent's phone. Not everyone had a house phone in those days. I certainly didn't. And mobiles hadn't even been invented. So the call would have been expensive. I probably paid for the call which had been well worth it anyway.

Round about then discretion should have kicked in but it didn't. I was, as I confessed before, rather naïve and now very excited.

So I told my mother my good news.

She had a conniption fit.

What was I thinking? Planning a future with a married man. No matter how divorced he was. He was too old for me. I didn't even know him. She reinforced her point ad infinitum and with some crude imagery. I listened a lot.

She made sense.

But I didn't need sense right then.

I needed a hug.

His hug.

(I probably need one now too! I miss them. I miss him.)

She was probably right in her views but I was happy. It took her quite some time to warm to him if she ever did. She had only met him briefly at my first husband's funeral when he had visited her house. It felt as if I had known him for forever.

When I got back home, I had two separate sets of feelings running parallel with each other. On the one hand I realised that I was in love. On the other hand I felt as if I was letting my family down…again.

And the memory of Gerry.

Would it be possible that these two parallel lines would ever meet?

No. Not ever. Or so I thought.

I paid *that* visit to the cemetery where Gerry was buried to finally put closure on 'us' and let him go.

So, then I wrote poetry to pass the time at night until Jack could arrange leave from work and come to visit. Well, I had been doing that anyway and needless to say the earlier stuff was full of moroseness and hostility and very doleful. Maudlin, I suppose.

The 'newer me' produced some nice love stuff.

Anyway, he arrived a couple of weeks later. The postman had started delivering his cards daily after the phone call so I was nicely kept company till his arrival.

A card a day keeps the doctor away.

Well, it worked for me!

He showed up one evening after the children had gone to bed. He flew from Riyadh to London to Dublin and hired a car to get straight to mine.

Ah lads the guilt!

Was nothing compared to the sensation of warmth that overcame me upon his arrival. He hugged better than anyone ever.

And it was all fairly tame.

We had coffee and chatted.

He told me he was an alcoholic 'in recovery' and that he had a number of years sobriety behind him. This was good.

He stayed at the local hotel.

That's what you did in those days. It was more proper. Until I had decided truly how I felt about him.

He came back the next morning.

Too excited to stay away.

Honestly he was like a big child.

Secretly, I was too. But a lot more held back. See, I was 'sensible' in those days.

So we had breakfast. The children were at school. We talked about them a lot. We were, after all, a package deal. Them and me.

So he became a quiet, friendly presence for a while getting to know them in stages. He liked them. They were no strangers to him since he had met them several times in years previously. And they were family.

But the day came when he had to go back to work.

We still hadn't been physical.

When he went back to the Middle East, I felt as if something was missing but I couldn't put my finger on it for ages.

Yep.

It was the intimacy we lacked.

So he sent flowers and cards. He wrote about his experiences in the desert. He sent me photos of growing things. He was a horticulturalist. A landscape engineer by profession. I loved his work. He was a specialist.

Soon enough he came back to Ireland. This time as a guest at a cousin's wedding.

He brought me along as a 'friend'.

Well, the wedding was great but the sex afterwards in his room was phenomenal.

Can't say more than that. I'm not that eloquent and my words wouldn't do justice to the feeling of being finally wrapped up in a love so warm and special it was like a blanket of desire and tenderness and rest. Like I had finally come home. And to his own surprise, amazement and deep, deep satisfaction, as if he had finally come home after so many years of wandering and disjointedness. He had an anchor. So did I.

We were officially and openly a couple.

He decided to take a sabbatical from his job. So we could get to know each other and he could bond with my family. Again, after some time, he had to go back to work in the Middle East.

Another separation.

But not before he proposed.

Of course I accepted.

There followed four months of torturous separation. During this time I joined the aforementioned church. Or prayer group. I found comfort there. To begin with.

But I pined.

We planned our nuptials over the phone.

I wrote more poetry.

I tore it up.

Finally we were married, in London as you know and my children and I could legally get residency in Riyadh.

As he had no leave left for that year, we travelled there by ourselves, two months later.

I'm still the same person that threw up a chance to study at Trinity in order to be closer to home and here I was travelling to Saudi Arabia.

In at the deep end!

Well, I trusted him that much.

I knew he wouldn't let us drown.

But it was over two months before we actually got to travel. I was getting pretty good at separations although they still hurt as much.

In February we flew from Shannon to Heathrow to Jeddah to Riyadh.

Thank God I had developed a bit of patience.

Four hours in immigration at the airport in Riyadh. Every resident of the sub-continent of India had decided to travel to Riyadh the same day I did. They literally packed the kitchen sink.

While he waited for us to come through the gate.

For four hours. Bless him.

So this country bumpkin turned into a real 'bona fide' city slicker.

This city was amazing. Except it was so totally fundamentalist Islamic.

Not that I had a problem with that. It actually suited me.

We were housed by the company in a very ordinary villa with a very ordinary pool and a very ordinary Pakistani driver. With very ordinary Filipinos as maintenance men.

There were several other similar villas in the compound, but were for the most part inhabited by employees of Rafia Hirara, multi billionaire and Jack's boss at the time we were in Riyadh. The other occupants of the compound were Middle Eastern. Great people. Predominantly Moslem. We got on famously.

We were fortunate in that the local British school had places for the three girls but Finn had to wait until the following September to join the reception year even though he had started school in Ireland.

So we enrolled him in a private kindergarten.

The Pakistani driver didn't really understand why he had now to do several additional school runs with these western children who were making his day very busy indeed. The trip to pick up Finn interfered with his siesta or 'prayer calls' I suppose. He had been an Olympian boxer who, I was informed, 'was more than a little punch drunk'.

After a while, though, we began to get along a whole lot better. But not until after I had several run-ins with him in the mornings. He did have a point, considering he had other children to drop to school from the compound. In several different locations in the city.

So that is how I overcame the problem of not being allowed to drive in Saudi.

You should have seen the face on him when I booked a shopping trip!

I gave up.

After that I shopped in the evenings with Jack and the children.

We made it a social occasion twice a week.

There are no pubs in Saudi.

Alcohol is prohibited.

The lack of either never bothered me anyway.

There are no cinemas.

But their shopping malls, even twenty odd years ago, were enormous and you could spend hours wandering around and marvelling at the abundance.

All things Saudi are ostentatious and over the top. Well, to a westerner like myself.

Hence the phrase 'Saudi Gaudi' was coined by some witty westerner before my time.

Everywhere were chandeliers. Gold plated shop fronts. Marble staircases. Polished everything.

So much bling!

We were dazzled by it everywhere we went.

Their gold souks are unreal.

Acres of stalls stacked high with as much gold and jewels that could be packed in.

The nice thing about Middle East gold is they are not allowed to sell or use anything less than eighteen carat. And prices were always reasonable.

One could haggle for reductions and probably get a bargain. Haggling was the norm. It was a very noble, honest way to do business. It was expected.

Gems were lustrous and plentiful and the souk attendants were usually kept very busy polishing and shining their wares. Well, in the Ar Rub Al Khali desert where there are flash sandstorms regularly, it had to be done.

Speaking of gold and jewellery, Jack had a friend whom he had met through his twelve-step programme called Cool Will.

Cool Will was an amateur jeweller and frequently came by to show off his latest acquisitions. He was a descendant of some Polish prince or other who had fled Poland at the start of World War Two. He had an unpronounceable surname. So he named himself Cool Will to help people remember!

Jack bought some pieces from him as presents for the children and me.

Jack looked on such purchases as investments. Not to mention the satisfaction of seeing the look on our faces when we were presented with our gifts.

I never really got into the whole wearing of gold thing until after he had gone. Then they became mementos to me of the times we had as a family unit in Riyadh.

Good times and fun times.

The nice thing about living as an ex-pat is you meet great people from all walks of life from around the world who become fast friends, since everyone is in the same boat in Saudi.

All are 'coagi's.' That is to say western outsiders.

Being a male westerner made a man a third-class citizen no matter what kind of a job he did. Being a western woman made one a fourth-class citizen in every Middle Eastern man's eyes.

'Camels and goats up front. Women in the back,' scenario. As the Saudi's travelled in their Toyota Pickup trucks.

Which proved very problematic when any kind of maintenance work had to be done around the villa. The woman of the house had charge of such things. It was unheard of for men to interfere in a woman's domain. The house.

I had to learn how to deal with the maintenance men on their level whether they were doing electrics or groundwork or whatever. It made me very precise in my instructions when describing what had to be done, otherwise they would walk off the job if I had not explained to them properly what I wanted done. Good training for life back home. In Ireland things like that were easier. At least we would have spoken the same language. Finally, I put occasions of wrath like that, from workmen, down to the language barrier and the fact that I was a 'coagi' and a woman at that.

There was no winning so I just got on with it.

Recreational activities were always 'fun times in the sun.' Whatever organisation or group planned the desert picnics, we could always be sure of a good day out.

If there was a fee, food and refreshments would be provided. If not, the practice was, everyone brought a dish or two or some kind of meat for the barbeque.

Those kinds of days were very relaxing and enriching to everyone.

They were lovely civilized days out and the ex-pat community flourished.

We had several parks and fairgrounds to choose from to visit at weekends. Generally the children spent a great deal of time in the pool. All students were given swimming lessons as part of the Phys. Ed. programme in the school, as well as gymnastics, music, drama and a wide range of extra-curricular activities. Free.

I mention life in Saudi because as time went by, I forgot about the many challenges life had visited on me, before Jack.

Much of this I attribute to the love of a good man and added to that the nice lifestyle we were enjoying, so I relaxed more and more as time went by.

If I had any forebodings at all I wrote them off as just my sense of the past raising its ugly head every once in a while.

But I was blissfully happy.

The children were doing well at school. Jack was busy at work and I was doing what I was good at.

Keeping house.

Jack was also changing. I was learning more and more about him as time went on.

He was acutely aware of his shortcomings in his earlier life and relationships.

He never criticised anyone for the situation he had found himself in so many years earlier. He had shed the anger that fuelled his drinking habit. He had made amends to anyone whom he had hurt in the past. He had moved on from his woes and had settled in nicely to family life, and as he called it, his second chance at getting it right. He was working his twelve-step programme.

He told me all his stories and I told him mine.

He told me all his adventures and I had none to tell him.

Apart from the one I was currently on with him.

He shared his difficult situation surrounding his first marriage.

When he failed in his efforts to be posted to Vietnam with his friend Toni, he stayed in Texas where they did their basic training. He worked out his enlistment as a chef for the Air Force in a Texan Air Force base. He was honourably discharged after serving out the requisite three years.

He had already notched up quite a few conquests with the ladies. He was popular and reckless.

The army nights were a riot of parties and booze. He told me that he had a problem with alcohol even then but was unwilling to admit it.

He eventually hooked up with a high-ranking officer's daughter. She got pregnant and so they got married.

And by then he was looking for regular work landscaping.

So they moved out west where the work and the money were.

Jack was quite excited about being a father. It was a new beginning for him and he really made an effort to be a good husband and father.

His role models were…

That was the problem.

He didn't really have any, unless you considered the Fallini family.

But they were a distant memory.

But he had no monkey to see and do except the one he carried on his back.

In all they had three children.

The marriage struggled along for years.

He had plenty of work.

He inherited his maiden aunt's money and they bought a house.

They were comfortably well off.

He behaved like single man. Partying and boozing.

She, of course, had to do it all.

Sounded so much like myself and Gerry.

I didn't judge Gerry for it.

Back in those days I was probably a better person than I am today.

Or maybe just more gracious.

Or maybe just naive!

The latter I'd say.

As I said the family struggled along for years. In the U.S. marriages were breaking down years before they were 'breaking down' here in Ireland. Divorce was a normal part of American society long before it started to happen here.

However, Jack was determined to keep his family intact. He worked hard. He stayed on the wagon for weeks on end. And fell off it too for weeks on end.

But the damage to his psyche had been prevalent for a long time. He was struggling with his demons and his propensity towards alcohol.

That's the polite way to say it.

Then one night after a twenty-four-hour bender he got in to his car and drove.

Obviously he was arrested and charged with being D.U.I.

He got six months in an open facility with community service. He was allowed to see his family every day but on this particular Friday as he commuted from work to see his children, he arrived home to be met with a brief note and part empty wardrobes.

They had left him.

Gone back to Texas.

And he couldn't even follow them.

He would be arrested and charged with greater offences if he left the county.

He had to wait out the remainder of his sentence in Marin County. He tried unsuccessfully to reach them by phone but her father wouldn't allow them to speak to one another.

A bit harsh you might say but being in the military it was her father's way for protecting his daughter.

He had been angling for this opportunity for a long time. He never did like Jack.

At the end of his sentence he went to Texas to be told they were over. She wanted a divorce. She wanted the house and sole custody of the children. She wanted children's maintenance.

Harsh, but Jack had no choice but to comply. The courts would uphold her requests since Jack was deemed unfit as a father. He had no recourse after his D.U.I. sentencing.

More losses.

Too many in one episode.

At work his bosses apportioned more and more of his duties to his fellow employees.

They had no choice. He was a felon. He had to work out his community service and he was unable to drive for the duration.

Family first.

Then his home.

Then work.

What next?

They say, we are never given more challenges than we can handle at any one time.

Jack had a good friend called Ed.

Ed worked in the Middle East.

Ed came back in to Jack's life round about then.

Ed was going to marry a girl from South Africa.

Her name was Eve.

Timing.

They were getting married. Jack was divorcing.

Jack met Ed and Eve for dinner one evening and before they reached the dessert course Ed had convinced Jack that he should try his hand 'greening the desert.'

Having nothing left to lose he started the job-hunting the very next day.

It wasn't long until he had secured work in Dammam, in the Eastern Province of Saudi Arabia.

So he left the States and travelled to Saudi Arabia after securing his visa and lodging the necessary paperwork with the Saudi Embassy.

It wasn't an easy decision, he would be leaving behind all he held dear, but he felt he had a better chance with his family if he were earning enough to treat them once in a while.

Second time in his life he had cut himself off from his family. Firstly he had no choice. Now he himself had made the decision, although reluctantly.

He figured if he wanted to leave the Arab country quickly all he had to do was strike a Saudi. Which he never had to do because he loved the Kingdom immediately.

He worked there several years building glasshouses and growing trees and shrubs for decorative purposes around that city.

Later he relocated to Riyadh where he supplied plants and landscaped the newly built airport there. So if you ever travel through the Airport in Riyadh, it was my Jack that was responsible for all those green living things and all the landscaping on the freeway leading out from the airport.

Working in the desert suited him.

He liked the heat. He liked working with a multinational workforce.

Of course he still needed time out and travelled quite frequently outside the kingdom.

It was on one of these visits that I first met him.

You know by now what happened thereafter.

Chapter 6

We lived in Riyadh two and a half years. We were extremely happy.

We decided to have a baby a year and a half into our residency in Saudi. Of course I had no trouble conceiving. As you know I had enough fertility for ten and so did Jack.

At the end of the first trimester I flew back home for our annual summer holidays with the children. Jack travelled several weeks later. He exited the Kingdom in the middle of August.

By the end of August in 1990 it was reported that Iraq had invaded Kuwait.

That wasn't good. Seen as an act of aggression towards its smaller neighbour the U.N. was obliged to intervene and it made demands on Saddam Hussein, the Iraqi President, that he should withdraw his occupying army from Kuwait or face the consequences and sanctions of the member states of the U.N.

That's what the U.N. does. It protects vulnerable nations from attack by stronger nations.

Theoretically.

That is why it was set up post Second World War.

While on vacation in the West of Ireland we listened intently to the news broadcasts being relayed hourly on television channels worldwide. For an ordinary person like myself it wouldn't impinge on my life much if it weren't for the fact that Saudi Arabia was bordering on Kuwait, so we considered our options. We would be living too close to the hostilities for comfort. What if Saddam Hussein decided to invade Saudi too?

Jack phoned a friend who was still in Riyadh and he said that everyone was 'cautiously optimistic' that the episode would resolve itself fairly soon. As our summer holidays were winding down, the situation remained at stalemate.

We decided to go back to the Kingdom since the children had to start school early September. Their fees were paid and were non-refundable.

But that wasn't solely our motivation. We were a family. Our home was there. Jack's work was there. Our child was on the way.

And if the powers that be there were 'cautiously optimistic' then we should be safe enough returning to Riyadh.

Riyadh is close to the Kuwaiti border so hostilities, if they did start, would be fairly close to home as I said. We were a little nervous returning but looked forward to getting back home and to normality. My mom fretted and worried. My brothers were neutral, preferring to allow Jack and I to make the decision to return to the kingdom. My dad as usual was quiet but wished us well.

In the end it was about us all being together. And going about our daily lives as usual.

You know hindsight is a great thing. Had we stayed at home for another five months we could have safely travelled back in to the Kingdom never having experienced the events of the start and finish of The Gulf War. But we needed to be together.

But because we, as a family, were threatened, I think of it as a crucial defining time in our lives.

Obviously it isn't so much fascination as tragedy for me. The children are still bemused by what went on in Riyadh during the final months of 1990 and the early months of 1991.

So we returned to Riyadh at the end of August. We tried to be as normal as possible. We still had friends over for dinners, went on outings to the 'goat grabs' in the desert, frequented the shopping malls and socialised as we always did. We did all the things we used to do.

But the school sent weekly updates regarding security of the children and staff at the school. It made me uneasy but I figured I was a little prenatal.

Some families were drifting out of the Kingdom as more and more troops were brought in. There began to be a heavier U.S. Army Personnel presence on the streets of Riyadh. It was becoming increasingly quieter out of doors at night time. An air of fear and uncertainty fell on the city as demand after demand from the U.N. fell on the deaf ears of Saddam Hussein and the Iraqi withdrawal from Kuwait was not happening.

We felt as if Stormin' Norman Schwarzkopf, James Baker, Sir Peter De La Billiere, and Colin Powell were old friends of ours. Their names were being bandied about so much on the Armed Forces Radio. The rattling of sabres continued for months on end. So now we were in a war zone!

Only I could accomplish that!

That's sarcasm by the way.

The situation became known as Desert Shield.

The combined forces of the US, Britain, France and several other N.A.T.O. countries, worked together for the security of the Gulf States against the might of the Iraqi army.

(I have to pull a lot of detailed information out of my memory banks right now.)

To most people the Gulf War is a distant memory. You have to be over thirty to remember the event, probably older.

However it is not ancient history.

It's recent compared with other major events in history, World War One and World War Two for example, and yet it has been largely forgotten by most people, but not by me.

Bearing in mind that I said earlier that I am an history buff and an history teacher I would find this episode in history fascinating, if I wasn't caught up in it.

The city, and indeed the region as a whole, was holding its collective breath.

I had decided to enrol in the University of Maryland to study Middle East History to distract myself and broaden my mind a little, and feed my brain cells. All the children were at school, so I had plenty of time. As I progressed with the pregnancy, I needed a house boy to do the housework. Unless you have lived or live in such a warm climate it's hard to imagine the heat, and what it can do to your energy levels especially when growing a baby.

I had already done a quilting course with the wife of the Canadian Ambassador and Chinese cooking with a Chinese chef's wife. So I thought why not study a topic on Middle East History. After all, I was living in the area. So I presented myself weekly at the American Community Services building to get lectures from Professor Grant Hack. Grant 'worked for the government' but had several degrees and post grad letters after his name so I presumed he was a genius. He was also one of the nicest people I had ever met and a superb teacher and I enjoyed his classes to no end.

And that kept me occupied mentally for a number of months.

Occasionally we went to the Irish Embassy to meet other Irish people. The Ambassador at the time was Brendan Lyons. His secretary was a Galway woman, married to an engineer. On one visit we met Gerry Collins who was travelling to Saudi probably on a fact-finding mission. He was the Minister for Foreign Affairs for the Irish Government back then. Trade agreements existed between Ireland and Saudi then and still do.

Normality slipped further away from us one day when Jack arrived home with gas masks and protective clothing in the event of a chemical attack. The only problem was we were allocated six gas masks but only two full chemical warfare suits. That left four of us unprotected from a chemical attack.

The 'cautious optimism' of a few months earlier was slipping away daily as the Iraqis stubbornly refused to withdraw from Kuwait. Several U.N. deadlines were ignored by the Dictator's Regime. Talk of Saddam Hussein having chemical weaponry capabilities, especially on Irish news broadcasts, were rife. My family were frantic with worry. They phoned regularly suggesting that we come home; that we were living in a dangerous situation. Try telling that to the gynaecologist I was attending. He wouldn't hear of it. Naturally one is not supposed to fly so close to the delivery date. Besides I didn't want to leave Jack and the children were enjoying school too much.

Jack, who had some friends who were also 'working for the government', didn't seem to be too worried. But I worried.

Especially when the children were requested finally to bring their gas masks to school.

Imagine the feelings that you would be experiencing if your loved ones were at a different location from you when a natural or unnatural disaster happened. So I sent them out to school every morning. With a lot of trepidation and these mundane questions...

Have you your lunch?

Do you have your E.C.A. money?

Did you pack your gas mask?

Of course I never did say this to my family back home in Ireland. We assured them we had the inside track on what was happening and that we were completely safe. God bless them, they were genuinely worried.

Jack and I, however, listened to Armed Forces Radio and Television Services.

On short wave radio if you're ever curious. We learned so much about propaganda. Not American propaganda you understand. The Arab states were mostly aligned with the western security forces which had been stationed in Riyadh. The Arab States do not recognise Israel. The only reference by the Arab to that race was 'those Mad Dog Israelis' Just as not all Arabs are Moslem. Not all Moslems are Arab.

Ariel Sharon, recently deceased was completely dogmatic on the issue. He would never countenance relinquishing any territory to the Palestinians who sadly do not have a state of their own. So many of our good Palestinian friends at the time, held no passports nor had a home country of their own. Mixed up politics and hatred like Northern Ireland or the Balkan states.

The UN security forces were stationed in Riyadh.

About half a kilometre from our villa.

Less probably.

We were sitting ducks really. A military installation is always a prime target, in time of war.

We watched from our balcony sometimes as planes multiplied daily at the local military air base. We watched with fascination as they manoeuvred or left the air base to carry out reconnaissance flights or 'recces' as they are called, to the Kuwaiti border on a daily basis.

We watched the Patriot missile batteries being installed.

Unnerving.

We made so many new friends as we 'adapted' an overseas service man or woman. A friend of ours met her husband during the period known as 'Desert Shield.'

We saw Saudi traditions blown away while watching American women soldiers driving 'hummers' and 'jeeps' through the streets of Riyadh.

The Saudi traditionalist Sunni Moslem leaders had to go into overdrive to reinforce the driving ban on its women at that time and afterwards.

It was my first introduction to Hum V's. If only they were left to their original function. Nowadays you can see that every sort of celebration in towns throughout Ireland is not complete without a Hummer. I find it all very comic, knowing what I do and how important they were to the war effort in 1991 in Saudi.

And a pink stretch Hummer! For the love of...

What can I say?

Enterprise.

So I passed my exam and got bigger by the day.

The kids had a sense of excitement about them. They were living through an adventure and I didn't want to spoil that for them.

November came and went.

We had to think about Christmas.

It was our first one away from Ireland. Although Saudi is a Moslem nation you could buy a Christmas tree and decorations in December. Practically anything that made a Christmas back home. We had a twelve-foot tree. It was amazing. We were resigned to being there and settled in for the season.

I couldn't travel anyway even if I was allowed. I would have needed three aeroplane seats. Customarily I was very compact when I was pregnant with my other children. Not this one.

The baby was due in January.

I was excited and restless.

The bigger I got, obviously, the less I slept.

There was an eerie atmosphere developing daily around the city. Families were going home.

Most of our friends had already left.

A sense of foreboding was growing over time.

The school decided to close shortly before Christmas.

'For the duration,' is how they put it.

So many families wanted to get away early on their holidays with the heightening of hostilities.

The embassies were advising evacuations.

The baby was due on the Fifth of January.

This was not good.

Jack was still going to work.

He was sleeping.

I was not.

He appeared not to be too worried.

I was just becoming more frayed at the edges.

I was now very big with child.

Christmas came.

They got their wish.

Boot skates.

I tried to talk them out of it. Reminded them that Cora had lost a front tooth to a footpath as a result of roller skating.

I relented.

Or Santa relented I should say or one of us did.

They were so amazing and graceful on their skates though.

I don't know what I was worrying about. They were happy. I often wish I could have mastered the art of fast flowing things like skating, ice skating, even skiing. But no!

They were brilliant.

They had ganged up on me and pleaded for the damned things.

Kids!

Again with hindsight I should have dug in. And not given in.

So they skated around the compound and swam in the pool and tried as best they could to busy themselves over Christmas and into the New Year.

All the Lebanese children had left the compound. So again it was just me and my 'brood'.

I was waddling around as best I could.

Being a housekeeper as best I could. Literally all things familiar seemed to be shutting down in Riyadh.

It was oddly cold and strange. The feeling and atmosphere is not easy to describe. In western movies when you see the tumbleweed you imagine 'ghost town.' Well, we expected to see tumbleweed at any time. The Armed Forces were still a visible force, but not much else to be seen.

We still went to the malls to shop. But there were less and less westerners obvious in Riyadh.

Most had gone home.

And the phone calls were still coming from Ireland. Why weren't we leaving? When were we leaving? Mostly from my brother Sid. I couldn't go home even if I wanted to. Nature had to take its course with my unborn.

The Pilipino caretakers came by and secured our house.

They taped our windows with plastic and scotch tape.

Great!

I felt so secure! That instilled confidence in me!

Scotch tape to combat chemical weapons.

Jack and I still tuned in to A.F.R.T.S.

But my family back in Ireland were listening to another channel.

The one that knows everything about everything.

No I'm not talking about RTE!

Talk about trying to balance the reality with the assumed, with a baby about to come into the world.

What they were worried about was that we would be poisoned when the Iraqis released Scud missiles towards Riyadh filled with poison gas.

As Riyadh was the capital of Saudi, with the primary air base for the region, we were wide open to the threat.

We were less than five hundred metres from impact.

Lovely.

If I opened my bedroom window, I could have had a conversation with the lads and ladies of the American Air Force.

Not good.

So I played it all down when they phoned. No! Not in any danger.

No, I lied regularly.

We are safe.

I hated lying to them.

They had lost enough.

I was a bad sister.

The whole town back home and the surrounding countryside was praying for us.

Thank God they were.

A sense of impending danger hung over the region. It was one of dread and fear and the atmosphere was contagious. It was commutable. There is such a thing as an ominous cloud which hangs over a situation like that. It was almost tangible at that stage.

Although it was winter, the cold in the evenings was nothing to the sense of foreboding that filled the city.

It was as if the inhabitants were waiting for something bad to happen.

Of course that's bad enough when you're somewhat comfortable, but being nine months pregnant there's no recourse to any comfortable situation.

I couldn't even find some relief in a night's sleep.

Every woman everywhere who's ever been pregnant will know what I mean. At nine months a full night's sleep is just a faraway dream.

It all was too much for me.

My Obstetrician, realising I was not resting or sleeping at home, brought me in to hospital on the third of January. Whatever chance I had of sleeping in my own bed at nine months, there was none in a maternity hospital.

The hard beds. The routine in the early morning. My doctor decided it was time I had the baby.

So on the fifth day of January 1991 I gave birth to Erin.

I loved her immediately.

But it was amid the fear of a threatening war.

I brought her home two days later, stopping along the way to have her photo taken for her passport.

We had battened down the hatches for chemical war.

I breast fed Erin as best I could. With foresight I had introduced the bottle early as I had to have a backup plan in case we were evacuated. She wasn't getting enough breast milk and liked to feed very frequently.

Of course I had no plans to evacuate when I brought my baby home.

It really all went pear shaped in mid-January.

No schools. Careful trips to the local shop.

Staying close to home for the best part of the day. Jack was still going to work.

The children were enjoying school free days. Since the other children in the compound had taken flight, mine had the compound all to themselves.

They had hours of fun with the Filipino maintenance men and even the driver joined in the odd game of 'snap.' They played Scrabble and I amazed myself at being so totally useless at the game as the Filipino whose first language was Tigalog, with English as his second language, always beat me.

They were getting better at the skating too. Even Finn who was only seven at the time was flying around.

Erin slept very sporadically and then only for thirty minutes at a time. She was an around the clock baby. Always up.

I wasn't resting at all. Always alert to her needs. Aware of trouble. It's what mothers do really.

One night when I was feeding her, I heard more than the usual activity of fighter engines from the nearby Military Air Force base.

Planes taking off.

Wave after wave.

The next day it was announced on A.F.R.T.S. that the combined forces of Desert Shield, having reached another ignored withdrawal deadline from Iraq, had launched an attack on Iraqi forces on the border of Kuwait. The offensive had started at five am.

That explained all the activity then during one of the night feeds.

Desert Shield had become Desert Storm.

We were under increasing pressure from all sides to move the family out of Riyadh amid the growing tensions. When the first air strike happened, I don't know which was worse, the threat of being bombed or the criticism we came under for keeping our family in a War Zone. I would love to have left but I could not take my child out of the Kingdom without an Exit Visa.

We were waiting for her passport to process since the day she came home from the hospital. Having secured that easily enough from the Irish Embassy, we then had to submit it to the Saudi emigration authority for approval to travel. I had mine and the others were permitted to leave but Erin could not. We waited and waited. All our passports were retained by the Saudi ministry of travel while we were in the Kingdom anyway. We were issued with an Igama or work permit which Jack was the holder of until we needed to leave the Kingdom. Then we had to apply for Exit Visas to get our passports back to travel out of Saudi. Law of the land.

When Erin was thirteen days old, we heard the first of the menacing air raid sirens sound over Riyadh.

And still no Exit Visa.

The sirens sounded after night fall.

That would have been bad enough but my second child Chris had taken a fall on her skates and broken her arm.

It wasn't pretty.

I was indoors feeding the baby when they all arrived in with Chris. Her femur was visibly broken all right. It was sticking out through her skin.

I threw up.

Usually I had a certain amount of cool about me if any of them got injured or were sick.

This was so bad though.

I was also fairly exhausted.

I paged Jack.

He came straight home.

He took her to Dallah Hospital.

I couldn't go obviously. I was not permitted to drive and someone had to take care of Erin and the others.

They x-rayed her and sent her home because she had eaten. Not that she needed an x-ray. It was fairly obvious but they did it to ascertain if there were any internal complications. Very reassuring for any post-natal mother, or any mother.

She had to go back in, several hours later, to have the bone set.

While she and Jack were in theatre at the hospital, the first of the air raid sirens sounded, in the theatre of hostilities.

The kids thought it was great.

I, on the other hand, knew the full ramifications of what was happening.

Audrey my third child, God bless her, thought it wise to pray.

The one remaining Pilipino came by to mind us, the other having taken holidays and had left a few days earlier for the Philippines.

It seemed like Audrey minded him.

Next thing we knew there was an almighty explosion. It nearly blew the door in. The percussion of the released Patriot missile was so severe.

Jack and Chris were still in the hospital.

He called me asking if we were ok.

He came home after the surgery leaving my precious Chris in hospital by herself.

But what else could have been done.

He knew I was already in shock.

The all-clear siren sounded.

Yes! There is such a thing.

So we came out of our safe room.

We chatted, ate some food and went to bed.

Chris was asleep and we could collect her the following day.

So I was somewhat relieved.

Still when your child is at another location and there's danger everywhere you never rest easy till you're all together.

It's a bit like in the movies.

Take the film The Day After Tomorrow for instance. The parent and child are separated and they move hell and high water to get back together. That's how it is.

Literally.

So movies like that bring it all back.

Vividly.

I couldn't wait to see her.

I had thought that they couldn't put her back together that maybe they would have to amputate and that her break was so serious it was unfixable. I had never seen anything like it. But it could have been her head that slammed into the wall of the villa. She saved herself by using her hand to take the force of the impact. The compound had tile as its walkways. The boot skates were high velocity ball bearing. She was probably travelling at some speed to do that kind of damage to her forearm.

Well, anyway we survived our first air raid. The phone calls came hot and heavy then.

When are ye leaving?

Why are ye still there? The pressure.

A small matter of an Exit Visa.

Then they closed down the airport.

What?

So how were we supposed to get out of Riyadh even if we did get the Exit Visa?

Our neighbours, the last remaining private aviation pilots were constantly on our case wondering when we were going to take the family out of the war zone.

Not them too!

My baby became known at the time as the 'Scud Baby.' As night after night we had several air raid warnings. The Scud Missile attacks went on for days and nights.

(Later a friend and I changed her name to the 'Patriot Baby.' Because the Patriot missiles defeated the Scuds.)

Finally, when she was three weeks old, we got Erin's Exit Visa.

Jack had to go to the top of his employment ladder to get it.

Hirara himself had to influence the authority in question. I suppose being considered a third-class citizen and a baby at that there was no rush on the said authorities to release an Exit Visa to her.

So on the twenty sixth of January we were offered a flight out of Riyadh.

If we wanted to take it.

To my dismay Jack could not leave his work.

Everyone else could have, so why not him.

Me and the children. Take it or leave it.

That was it, no compromise.

Jack insisted we go.

A few days earlier a number of servicemen in the installation in Dammam had been killed when a Scud missile scored a direct hit on their barracks.

I hadn't slept for days.

Air raid sirens were sounding nightly and sometimes twice, maybe three times and more at night, which meant we had to get up and go to our safe room.

I was totally exhausted and edgy from the constant interference with our sleeping patterns.

Erin didn't have a chance to settle. She was woken regularly.

The routine was as follows…

The air raid siren sounded. We went to our safe room. You could hear the whistle of the incoming Scud missile. Then the loud percussion of the Patriot battery deploying its missile. The door of the villa shook tremendously every time. Then somewhere a pop as the Patriot missile released from our neighbouring Air Force base blew up the incoming Scud somewhere over Riyadh. A meteor shower of molten metal shrapnel then fell to earth anywhere over Riyadh. Dangerous in its velocity it was unwise to be caught out of doors.

Then the all-clear siren. Then back to bed.

Try to get back to sleep.

The shock of the broken arm coupled with childbirth and air raids convinced me that Jack was right.

So we opted to go home.

We packed a few bags and headed towards the Irish Embassy.

As this was an evacuation, we had to get our instructions there and our paperwork processed through the Embassy.

We were then driven through the back streets to the closed airport.

Sitting on the tarmac of the private aviation section was a Hercules jet.

The American Air Force was flying a number of flights daily in and out of Riyadh for supplies and such, and they were taking off literally as soon as we arrived at the private aviation area of the airport.

We said our hasty goodbyes to Jack and boarded the aircraft. There were several other evacuees on board that flight that day. All tired, all apprehensive like we were.

We were not informed of our destination.

We could have landed at any city in the Middle East or Europe or even further afield.

I was relieved to be out of the war zone but this new twist to the tale really bothered me.

I had four very tired individuals and a three-week-old baby. Jack was in Riyadh out of reach even by phone.

What to do?

Hercules jets are made for troop transportation and freight.

There are no seats.

We sat in the hammock style seats.

There was no toilet.

Just a urinal at the front of the aircraft.

For men.

Fully exposed. The urinal that is.

Thankfully we touched down at Luxor airport.

A toilet break.

But what a toilet.

There was one cubicle.

Sticking out of the toilet was some kind of metal rod, as if someone had tried to flush a coat hanger down the toilet.

The entire duty-free section of the airport was devoted to Le Creuset pots and pans.

After we had carefully done our business we got back on the aircraft, with military escort, mind you, and headed to another unknown destination. Most of this journey was through military air space. Meaning we were flying at risk.

Some of the payload had been taken off the Hercules Jet as we were enjoying all the 'luxuries' that the terminal building in Luxor had to offer.

A few weary hours later we touched down in Rome's Da Vinci Airport.

It was the smoothest touch down I had ever experienced up to then and thereafter.

They must get some training on those Jets or maybe it's the design of the plane itself.

Anyway we were greeted at Rome's terminal building by a hoard of what can only be described by the nowadays modern term: 'paparazzi.'

Cameras in our faces, everywhere.

Reporters with microphones.

Audrey, ever the actress, stole the show. She made it on to Italian television.

This was the adventure of their lives.

We were still committed to security and so my own answers were vague.

Besides I was too tired for it all.

Several of the Irish travelling group were assigned to the same hotel as the children and me. The others were installed in other hotels. We had one thing in common.

We were all exhausted and needed to get back home.

A representative of the Irish Embassy in Rome and an Aer Lingus official met us and informed us that we were being flown back to Ireland the next morning.

Early.

We got in to our beds at midnight. I was up at four.

Feeding time and nappy duty.

Then I called the others and got ready to leave for the flight back to Ireland.

We were being flown to Shannon, and were due to arrive by midday. I made a hasty phone call to my brother Sid from the hotel, in Rome, and we were on our way.

Aer Lingus could not do enough for us.

As evacuees we got escorted through customs. Through queues. And were installed in seats right next to each other. We had every service laid on. Kudos to that airline.

As we walked through the terminal building in Shannon, heads turned as we walked through customs with airport police and yellow ribbons on our luggage. We couldn't have been more obvious if they had spray painted our foreheads with the word 'evac.'

Back in Ireland, I could tell that the brothers and my parents were relieved.

So was I.

But Jack was still in a war zone.

Another loss?

I hoped and prayed not.

I was still not sleeping.

(To this day Erin is an up all-nighter.

And so amazing to boot. Alert!)

So we watched the news each night.

There was a different type of news being fed the Irish than we were used to in Riyadh.

There was so much speculation and scaremongering, was it any wonder the family were concerned.

But back in Riyadh we knew that the American Patriot Missiles had the situation covered.

There were a number of minor impacts from scuds but there was only that one which had any major impact, the one I mentioned earlier, in Dammam.

Cool Will used to go outside in his underwear to view the impact strikes. They lit up the night sky and the light of falling, molten debris was like a fireworks display, is how he described it.

We made a joke about that too. He was some light relief in the midst of the trying times we shared before we were evacuated.

He took pictures. I have one on my study wall as a reminder of the reality which is now a memory.

He was able to tell us that there was no such capability in the Iraqi arsenal to deliver chemical weapons from Iraq to Riyadh and that Scud missiles were too short range to carry such a payload that distance. Scuds therefore were empty missiles.

Bless him.

We were too far out of range.

But they did do some damage in the city, as they fell to earth, so we never could relax fully.

So it was February and with no sign of the ending of hostilities, I sent the children back to their old schools. They were greeted with a mixture of feelings from their old friends. They settled in and then towards the end of February the combined forces of Desert Storm completely overcame the 'might' of the Iraqi army. The war ended and Jack was safe.

The amount of destruction left behind by the mobilised Iraqi army was tremendous.

They set fire to oil wells along the Kuwait border with Saudi Arabia and when we returned to Riyadh a pall of smoke descended on the city and hung around there for months.

Back in Riyadh, we went on with our lives.

The schools reopened.

People who had left started to drift back to the kingdom.

Jack got busier and busier.

I still had no sleeping pattern established by the time we left the Kingdom for good that August.

Jack had used up his annual leave to come to Ireland to fetch us back in February.

Obviously I was tired travelling back and forth that year. We couldn't stay in Riyadh during the summer break. It would have been too long and too hot and too much for the children.

I needed a pattern.

Erin needed to settle.

So Jack and I chatted about our situation quite a bit before making the decision.

Fees had to be paid.

Were we sure we wanted to stay another year?

Cora was required to wear the 'abaya.'

That ugly black bag thing that girls of a certain age had to start wearing!

She already had a 'run in' with a Mutawa, or religious police type person, wielding a stick.

We wanted to get her and the others back in to the Irish school system.

Basically we wanted to go home and settle down.

So that is what we did.

I suppose I have expanded uncharacteristically with that episode in my life.

But it isn't everyday a girl gets caught up in a warzone.

Audrey and Chris always regret that we had to come home.

Finn didn't like the heat and wasn't too bothered.

Cora was glad to be back at school, not having to wear the abaya and getting ready for secondary school.

I needed normality.

So we came home in August nineteen ninety-one.

We bought a house.

Finally.

Somewhere we could call our very own.

But for Jack it had a tremendous significance.

He was back.

After decades of trying to find himself, he was reconciled to his natural family.

His sobriety was going well.

He had a new family.

He had a baby.

He had a wife who was Irish. He was finally home.

When Erin was one year old my mom died.

I was so upset. I had spent weeks doing nights at her house. I would take out the local newspaper and read it to her as she fell asleep. The brothers had put a second bed in her room and I slept there a couple of nights a week.

I missed Jack on those nights and I missed Erin. Of course the older children were well taken care of by Jack, but I wanted to spend time with my mother whom I had missed while we were living abroad. I think we finally made peace with one another during those last months. It's as if I, like

Jack, had been a displaced person for years. But now I was enjoying our times together as if the previous twenty odd years had dissipated. I wish she could have had a better life. I wished she could understand how happy I had been raising my children and being away with Jack.

My mother was so special.

No one could deny that.

In spite of the hand that life dealt her she always had time for others. She was a great mother and always did the best she could and if anyone needed anything, she was so giving. Even as I write this I can think of numerous instances when she went out of her way to make people feel better about themselves. She always had an open-door policy that would put many to shame for their selfishness. That wasn't her ulterior motive. She was happy just to see other people happy. She usually bore the brunt, physically, of the visiting 'townie' cousins. But she would treat them all as her own and there was always a bed for them and dinner on the table for the numerous cousins as they descended on the homestead each summer and at holiday times. She practically reared several of the 'citified' relatives.

Truthfully, she was all that and more. She didn't deserve to be stricken with anything except good health and a long life. However that's not the way things pan out for some people.

She had amazing courage and humour.

She was also beautiful.

In her heyday, I'd say she was statuesque and strong.

She gave up a good career as a nurse in Scotland to be with my father.

They met and fell in love and were married within six weeks as you know and then she had all of us.

If it were nowadays at least they would have the benefit of contraceptives. But I can't imagine my life without my little brother or my older ones.

Then they had my grandmother.

God help us.

I haven't been very nice about her although to be fair she had it hard too, but she overused her mental strong-arm tactics on my parents.

Definitely misplaced.

Another Maud Gonne type.

So we came home to stay.

We settled back in to Ireland beautifully, although neither one of us was working and the income would have come in handy. We were living off our savings. We hadn't much of that. How could we with five kids and flying back and over to Saudi on account of the war? And I didn't work.

Later, after my mother died, I was back in college and had taken on the H. Dip. as it was known back then. Jack was amazing doing the stay-at-home parent, but in the summer of the Dip. year we had realised that he had to get a job. Not everyone wanted to employ a 'fifty something' even though he had a resume that was seriously reputable, so he decided that he needed to go back to work in Saudi.

Oh no. This was not good. I was frustrated having to even consider it let alone make a decision like that.

He had to go to London to meet with his recruiter.

He came back a couple of weeks later. He spent a while in London visiting his friend. I hardly recognised him.

He had lost weight and didn't look so good.

I begged and pleaded with him to go and see a doctor. He assured me all was well. Why are men so 'thick'? (For want of a better word.) About their health that is.

Soon thereafter, I got my first job teaching in the local boy's school, earned my first pay check and Jack was so proud of me. There was no interview. Thankfully, it followed on from doing my teacher training in that school.

I was proud of myself. At least now one of us was earning an income. We could relax a little.

We were enjoying our friends. We had a social life which came from joining a local drama group. It was a lot of fun. He did the sets and I had these minor character roles.

He was always making something for the sets. He was a handy man.

Of sorts.

I was so happy to get a job. I don't know why I was. It seemed like the most normal thing to do after being a full-time mother for fourteen years. I seemed to just segue into it like slipping on an overcoat. One minute I was 'housewife of the year' the next I was 'career girl.' Maybe that was the power of the Higher Diploma that I had been doing. Goodness only knows how I transitioned that easily. I really enjoyed working in the all-boys school where I did my teacher training.

But as I said, he didn't look so good when he came home from London that September. He tried to reassure me that everything was okay. Everything was not okay. Did he think that I was blind?

Or stupid?

I was accustomed to action. Not this, 'I'm okay' bullshit. I insisted he go to a doctor. He insisted otherwise. If we weren't so happy, I'd say that's the closest we ever came to an argument.

That's right. You can be happily married and never have an argument. We didn't. Sounds impossible, but it's true. What had we to argue about? We 'got' each other totally.

Finally he relented around the end of November. Two lost months of medical care.

He was sent straight to hospital for tests. He was told all the bad news while he was there on his own. That hurt nearly the most.

I should have been there with him when they told him what he had. Lung cancer, from a lifetime of cigarette smoking.

I was working, I think, or busy with the kids. Anyway they should have held off until I got there. Knowing him, he probably insisted, thinking it would be easier for me if he told me himself.

But he was so sweet when he told me the results.

'A bit of chemo and I'll be fine.'

'No. no, no, no, no, this can't be happening.'

Just when everything was falling into place, well nearly.

We were home. He was home finally after forty-three odd years. He was home and that was a defining time in his life. I had said to him once at the outset of our relationship that I had something he needed. I had meant that with me he would have a home, an actual home in Ireland, no matter where we were, because of my Irishness. And of course he wholeheartedly agreed.

His Ex had told him that before they had ended the last time. She had said to him that he had unfinished business in Ireland. Little did she know or maybe she did.

And now, years later, we were happily settled and he would have been working sooner or later.

Cigarettes. How I kicked the habit.

A year later Erin started asking questions like, 'Why did my daddy die?'

Since I couldn't lie to her, I told her the truth.

He smoked.

He got lung cancer.

She was wondering if the same thing would happen to me.

Yes, I was still doing the thirty a day back then.

So, because she put two and two together and came up with worry, I kicked the habit there and then.

The most effective quit smoking tool ever.

That and Cora ranting on about the stinking smell of smoke in the bathroom every morning after I'd been and had my first cigarette of the day. Of course that went on for months but Erin had it wrapped up. She was too innocent to fool.

All hats off to them for their one hundred per cent success rate at getting their mum to quit smoking.

It was the perfect pincer manoeuvre. I'd swear they were in 'cahoots.'

Well, back in the Irish school system the reality set in. Audrey and Chris had missed out academically more so than Cora and Finn and they were struggling with Irish, rote learning and friends. I'd say if they ever wrote their own memoirs, they would have a tale or two to tell about their experiences back in their old school. Suffice it to say for now they were extremely challenged. The death of their stepfather didn't improve their ability to make or keep friends even then. They had such great experiences in their school in Riyadh that they were utterly dismayed by the antics of certain individuals they encountered back home, and they were not all students.

So as Jack ran down the clock to his demise all I could do was wait and watch him deteriorate. That Christmas we had decided I wouldn't go to the hospital on Christmas Day, where he was having chemotherapy, that I should stay at home and make everything as normal as possible for the children. We did all the Christmas Morning stuff. Opened presents. Called Erin to open her Santa presents. Yes, Erin had to be called every Christmas morning to open her Santa presents.

Every Christmas.

No such thing as her being up at five. Nightly she was awake late and I had exhausted nearly all my fairy tale stories on her by the time she was three. The little pigs' story had become something of a real estate anomaly. I talked her through three types of porridge in my sleep and yet she was wide awake at midnight. In the morning she was at her least energetic and all five of us had to literally scrape her off the bed each Christmas morning to open her presents.

She was the one remaining Santa user in the house at that stage, if you get my meaning!

That final year, when Jack was still with us, she was a boy.

Denis Irwin to be exact.

She would not entertain wearing a dress for love nor money. So we dressed her, at her request, in boy clothes for a whole year.

No hair ties.

Nothing pink.

Shoes, not pumps.

Then, on this particular Christmas Eve when Jack was so ill, she wanted a dress. Nothing would do her unless she got a dress. Quite out of the blue, she was a girl. She'll probably kill me for sharing this. But her siblings thought it so endearing. Like when she was a baby, they called her 'the guppy' because she opened and closed her beautiful pink baby mouth like, what we would call in Ireland, a goldfish.

So I trawled through the shops on Christmas Eve while on my way to visit Jack in the oncology ward in the hospital and finally found one which remotely resembled something she would wear. We all know shopping last thing Christmas Eve is fraught with disappointment since so much of everything has been sold out of the shops. It was probably the last dress in all of the city and surrounding areas but she loved it and transitioned into a girl so easily having been a boy for a whole year. I got it in Dunnes, by the way. She made me take a photo of her Christmas morning wearing her new dress and being a girl. She dressed herself, and then proudly strode into our living room while posing with arms wide questioning, 'Am I gorgeous?'

She wasn't yet four.

It was a blue sapphire sweep dress, lacy underskirts, with a velvet, black Bodice. I remember it so vividly. Of course she had no objections to wearing the lovely black patent shoes I bought her on that same shopping expedition.

So we know all about Shiloh Jolie Pitt being a boy. She insists on dressing as a boy and having short hair. Erin liked her long, curly, blonde locks thankfully.

Totally natural.

Nowadays, Erin is the most elegant of women.

Much like her older siblings.

Excitement over, I put my turkey into the oven to cook and started preparing the vegetables that Christmas Day.

Then I got a call from the hospital.

'Can you come in?'

'Oh God I hope he is okay! Let him be okay.'

So I took my turkey out of the oven, put it into the boot of my car. Loaded up my five brave children and dropped them off at my cousins' house. They were on permanent standby anyway ever since I told them Jack was terminal.

So on that particular Christmas Day I found myself on the road to the hospital.

It's not that he was any worse or declining, someone had decided to override our decision and drag me away from my children to be with him on the one day of the year that they didn't want their patients to be without their loved ones.

Jack was pissed that I had been sent for and that our plan was overridden.

Well, so long as I was there with him, I was happy. And so was he.

Eventually I pulled myself away.

I knew every drug that was known to man which had to be used to get him through. When he came out of the hospital in early January, I was able to administer the morphine myself and other drugs which I care not to mention. To see a loved one being this dependant on another person is hard. This man who had walked the earth during some of the most testing times anyone could have, being reduced to the state that he was in, made me feel helpless. I cannot imagine how he felt.

And then he slipped away ever so quietly one Friday evening in January just before his birthday. He had been taken to the local hospital to get some respite with the local Cancer Care people.

He was gone within hours.

The unit has since closed down. Honestly I don't know what our local and national politicians do be thinking of.

Bad grammar moment!

This facility meant everything to the local community.

Personally I think our former government were a bunch of Marie Antoinettes. They played all day with their big shot friends and were completely unaware of what was going on at ground level.

If any one of them had taken the time to walk down the high street of any small town in Ireland or driven through the mounting building sites around these small towns, they would have figured out that the country was in so much trouble economically.

But they would probably have been too thick to get it.

Jack and I always wondered what happened to all the tax money people paid. We still had potholes in the roads. We didn't have beautiful civic amenities. Our health system was third world even back then. It's gone to pot entirely now. I feel for the nurses and doctors who are at the coalface. They work so hard. I won't even start on the education cutbacks. And to have even one person homeless in Ireland puzzles me entirely.

Anyway these Marie Antoinette's thought we were all in possession of the same 'cake' they were on. No! Not likely. While they played their little milkmaid games with their cronies, they were blind to the inevitable. As if they gave a shit.

I did say my mind wanders sometimes.

A week after Jack died so did one of my brothers. His name was Joe.

Accidental death. He was the outdoors type. The farmer's son to help my dad with the farm. One day, while working on an animal in a cattle crush, a well-aimed kick from the animal to Joe's head rendered him lifeless. No way back for him either. His death was instantaneous. Thank God my mum wasn't alive.

Another funeral. A week after Jack as I said.

I went back to work a couple of weeks later.

Then another brother died. Pete found himself at the wrong side of a lorry being left out of gear in the yard. He was usually so careful. My poor father was inconsolable.

Accidental death. (Again thank God she was gone.)

Pete. Two months after Jack.

I didn't even have Jack with me to help me through the trauma of their deaths. I was numb from his going anyway.

Are their different degrees of grief?

I'd like to know.

There's the shock of someone's death to begin with.

Then there's the numbness.

Then the 'why?'

Then the anger.

There is always much crying.

Especially at night.

Grief.

Yes, I've had tons of it.

I'm sure there are similar stories out there.

My mother had gone by then.

Like I said, just as well.

I can't imagine how she would have coped with it all.

She probably would though.

Coped.

Somehow.

She rests with her three sons and her husband now.

Let me tell you about, what I call, the 'Soft' here.

I reckon I owe it to you all now.

The 'Soft' is a peculiar place. You hang out there long enough you feel like you get invisible. Although you are the most visible person on the planet because everyone you know and don't know have you in their sights. Because of your losses. I had lost Morgan. Gerry. Jack. Joe. Pete. My mom.

In the 'Soft' you are conducting soft conversations. People touch your hand softly. They ask soft questions: you give soft answers. It's what has to happen after a traumatic event. Only I didn't know at the time that I was going through the soft what it actually was. Now I know it was a time of not living consciously. It's where you find yourself with no choice. It's what grief looks like and feels like.

It's what it does to you and to other people who are there with you and taking that journey with you. Be they family, close friends or all the way over to just casual acquaintances.

I had to pull myself out of the 'Soft.' Like a science fiction movie where the aliens are the far side of a force field and you can, if you want to, dip in and out of their world.

The 'Soft' was alien to me despite the fact that it was so comfortable.

I would like to have the 'Soft' about me all my life but unfortunately it only comes with sadness and loss.

So I pulled myself into the 'Hard'. A word I will try not to overuse.

Reality. That is. And I hated every second I had to become real. Adaptable. A survivor. But the 'Soft' was killing me.

I'm a reality person. My home place. It worked for me all those times of grief. It works for me now too.

Why am I saying this?

Because someone might get some comfort from what I am illustrating from my life.

Sometimes reality sucks but the flip side is numbing.

So numerous times in my life I have had to bid farewell to the 'Soft' and move myself to the hard, harsh reality of living with and living without.

Today I am remembering the twenty second year of Jack's death.

So at times such as these I want to creep back into the soft but it is not feasible.

My offspring would worry and fret. So I can't have that.

I actually love the 'Hard'. It works for me totally. I feel conscious, alive, vibrant, successful and in tune with the universe.

I get bothered for people who spend too much time in the 'Soft.' And they expect everyone else to do likewise.

Only because I cannot do it for too long and sometimes I feel as if I am being judged for liking reality better than the 'Soft.'

Yes, people think I should be in the 'Soft' the whole time, knowing what I know. Having experienced what I did. Done what I have done. Been where I've been.

'That's the 'Soft.'

So what in comparison is the 'Hard?'

It's what got me off my butt every morning, out the door, doing the daily reality of life.

Did I feel like it?

No.

I felt like curling up into a ball. Hiding in the 'Soft' which required little effort. But I pulled myself out of the ether of grief gradually for the sake of my family and myself.

That transition was not easy. But it had to be done.

'Get busy livin' or get busy dyin'. Shawshank Redemption.

Reality is the best place to be. The best place for me.

So I put too much effort into reality and too little into doing nice things.

Because I have had to be one hundred per cent functional, I haven't had too much opportunity to be creative or had much chance to enjoy the finer things in life until recently.

Someone asked me lately, 'What's it like to be a woman of leisure?'

Damned if I know.

I have never known what being at leisure looks like or feels like.

Even now I am the frontline of family and work schedules and demands. If I am not currently nine to five does not mean I am a woman of leisure. I really don't want to be one. Ever.

So having lost two husbands, three brothers and my beloved mother. I had to pull myself into the 'Hard.'

Reality.

Chapter 7

So I busied myself with living again.

More losses.

So is there anyone keeping score. At this point there's no point. It's all run in to one very unfortunate past for me. I miss them all. I still do.

I changed schools and got taken on in a lovely local school about ten minutes' drive from my house. I had landed on my feet as they say. The children stayed in the schools they were in. Erin was just starting primary.

Honestly she hung out of my leg every morning for a whole year as I was attempting to say goodbye to her and be on time for my own job.

I say this to my friend a lot when she needs encouragement. If I can do it, so can you.

She's newly divorced.

I think I was an emotional fish for the best part of ten years. I was on automatic pilot.

Well, I couldn't put it down for a minute. When I say 'it' I mean responsibility.

I had no depressive tendencies since my late twenties so I am happy to report, for me it didn't come back.

But I had very little fun.

All the sociable things I used to do with Jack went by the wayside. There was always too much to do.

Saturday, washing the uniforms.

Sunday evenings, ironing the school uniforms.

Friday through Monday making sure the homework was done, the dinners cooked, the house was in order. Bills had to be paid. P/t meetings had to be attended. There was no end to it. I look back and I can honestly say it was probably a very happy time for me once I had dealt with the grief. It was a simple time. I was busy. I was always on call. I remember a time when I had to drop one of them off in a morning doing summer work at eight am. And pick up someone else at twelve thirty at night from summer work. I was, at times, living in my car. All the while Erin was in national school, I had to make sure she had a lift in the morning if I couldn't bring her and one in the evening if I wasn't back from work to collect her from school. I mention this so that all those wonderful people out there who helped me out should be commended. We really cannot do without the help of others. As the poem goes, 'No man is an island, entire of itself.' John Donne.

Well, whatever sacrifices I had to make it's been worth it all to be a mother to my children.

And although nobody's perfect, we're perfectly happy with one another.

Back to the task at hand.

Work.

Remember I said that I loved my job.

Well, it's true.

Cora says and to quote Confucius…

'If you love your job, you'll never work a day in your life.'

A job can keep you sane as in my case or drive you crazy as in my case.

You see the work itself was never a problem for me. I can work till I drop. It's what the job turned into in the latter years of my teaching career.

A good colleague and friend of mine told me lately it's quite common to 'go off' the teaching, when you come to that point in your career and you know it's over.

'But I wasn't at it that long,' I reminded him.

He looked at me and said, 'yes but you've been busy with other things all your working life and before.'

It's true. And I had to be reminded of that fact.

And you see I always counted myself a mother first a teacher second.

It's not that I was in and out and up and down and all that. In actual fact I took very few sick days and probably no discretionary days for years. It's only when mine started to graduate that I took some days out.

So I figured it was time to go.

I could relate some wonderful stories of my teaching days and not so wonderful stories, besides.

I could also wax lyrical about all my colleagues. I could and should mention my former boss and his Deputy Principal.

It was like going home just going to work.

So as wonderful as the lifetime of my work was, so in a way the displeasure I was feeling towards the end made me full of wonder.

Most of what I liked towards the end was the opportunities which I took producing school shows.

I really wanted to facilitate young musicians, dancers, singers, actors. Holistic education it is called.

Sport was facilitated.

Art was facilitated.

I zoned in on talented teenagers and those that could benefit from a good dose of the stage.

I had the most amazing musical director, my best friend Annie.

The most prevailing regret of my personal life is that I never got the opportunity to study music in any great depth. I love music. All sorts, as you know.

So I lived out my own musical shortcomings vicariously through anyone that wanted to have a go.

In a positive sense of the word.

Exhausting rehearsals.

Opening night.

Closing night.

Ah what a blast.

Chapter 8

God really held back with the game plan for me I think. On more than one occasion too!

Although roughly ten years ago, I decided to take matters in my own hands.

Not consciously though.

I had been asked out for coffee.

So I decided to go. This was after I had pulled myself and my family away from the aforementioned 'prayer group'.

His name was Al.

Here is how that episode in my life goes.

I had been telling my cousin, my confidante, that I had met someone. I called him 'the dinner person' because when you don't want to go places in your head with a relationship what's the best thing to do? Call that someone 'the dinner person' of course. So Al was 'a dinner person' for months. And then all of a sudden, we were engaged. I can't say how that happened. I expected it would have happened anyway but not when it did and not with the speed at which it did. As far as I am concerned, I had committed anyway and what's a ring and a ceremony between friends. But he was determined to hold on to me. Besides I guess he knew he had a bit of competition and he couldn't risk losing me. To my mind there was no one but Al for me. He was the one. Mr Right.

What was that question I was asked at that long-forgotten interview?

I have a very good friend. He says to me, 'providence is a rule of thumb.' He tells me the loveliest story of when he met his wife. He was playing a late-night gig in some pub in County Cork somewhere, with his band. They had finished the gig, but the bar owner asked them to play a little longer. Not thinking anything of it they stayed to play a few more songs. The next thing you know she walked into the bar and he had seen and fallen for his future wife. Just like that. They hit it off straight away. They have been married for over forty years, still as in love as ever. Providence.

That's Mr and Mrs Right.

And here am I still trying to get to year ten. However I have beaten all my own records and celebrated ten years of marriage this year to Al. I tell people Al is a real risk taker. I suppose it's not funny but we both know how fortunate we are that providence has smiled on us.

(The story of our getting together from Al's perspective.)

Al spent a lot of time trying to convince his son Carl that his relationship with me, was real…

Carl was not happy. Al was not happy either.

They were having a flaming row about Al's good news. Carl of course didn't see it that way.

'You can't be serious dad.'

'I am serious Carl'

'But it's too soon.'

'What measure are you using Carl to gauge what's too soon and what's the right time. The right time for me is now.

I'm so lonely since your mother died. I'm not functioning anymore like I should. I'm lonely Carl and Cathy is the only one for me now. I can't live on my own anymore. I can't do it. It's too painful. I loved your mother with all my heart. Nothing I can do will bring her back. So don't you see I have to go on living? And without someone by my side I will not be living. I will be lost. She understands me. She's been through the same as me. She has no agendas, Carl. I guarantee you that. We are good together.'

'What about Daniel and Rick? They're furious.'

'Well, your brothers will just have to accept the situation. I can't just crawl under a rock and die. I'm still a young man. Everyone deserves a second chance at happiness.'

'That's true but it's far too soon to commit to another woman after mum.'

'No Carl it's not. Not for me. What do I have to say to convince you that I have to do this? To get on with my life. She has been on her own for ten years. She needs me too. Although she has managed on her own till now. I doubt she would have accepted me if she had any doubts about my feelings. She gets the whole bereft thing Carl. There aren't many women who would. And I've known her all my life. I know her family. She knew your mother. She is genuine Carl, I just know it. Please say you understand. Please. And tell your brothers she is good for me. I need her.'

'Dad, you have to slow down.'

'No Carl I can't. I am a lonely man. How often do I see you? And when you do come home you spend more time with your friends. Not that I mind, but you have your lives. And I have mine.'

Carl was flying back to London and had to leave it at that but he still managed to hug his dad and tell him that he loved him.

'I'll call you soon dad.'

With that he got into his hired car and drove away.

The older man was disappointed.

Disappointed but happy.

He had been given a second chance at being happy.

He had to take it.

He could see no other alternative.

He thought of all the times he asked me out for coffee but he knew I was considering for a few months before giving him an answer.

Actually as it happened, I got back to him and asked him out for coffee.

Feck it if I wanted to feel in control, that was fine with him. He remembered me from his youth.

He described remembering me from our younger days as dark skinned and beautiful. I had brown eyes and at that time I had dark hair. Years before. Then I went off to college and got married to some farmer. Next thing he knew I was a widow. Then I was widowed a second time. He couldn't imagine how one person could absorb so many shocks and survive, and to top all that off I had lost brothers but he couldn't say how many.

But he still considered me as the same girl he remembered from his youth.

Some people have really a hard time and although he himself had suffered he couldn't imagine what life must have been like for me.

He was thrilled when we made our first coffee date. We arranged I would come to his house to meet up only because I knew him well. Normally I would be more cautious.

So when I opened with the line, 'I thought we were going to meet at Greys for drinks last week. Where were you?'

'Were you there?'

'Yes, I waited for you. But that's okay I met someone.'

'Man or woman?'

'A friend. We chatted.'

'So how did that go?'

'Really well, but I would have preferred if you were there and hadn't stood me up.'

'I didn't think you would meet me.'

'Generally I say what I mean and I do what I plan, unless it compromises the safety of my children.'

'Oh.'

'Speechless are we?'

'Well, yes. Sorry about that.'

'Well, I'm here now.'

'I'm glad you came.'

'Oh yeah?'

'Yes. I'm glad you came.'

'Actually so am I.'

'Where's all the family?'

'They don't live here anymore, all moved away.'

'So we have the house to ourselves then?'

'Yes, we do.'

'Well, why don't we just stay here, rather than go out for coffee?'

'That's fine if that's what you want to do.'

'Well, unless we travel fifty miles from here and have luck on our side, the whole town won't know our business. I'm not in the mood right now for answering questions and raised eyebrows.'

Al was only too delighted to stay put. He had had a long day at work and was just as happy to relax by the fire.

'I'll put the kettle on for a cup of tea,' he said, 'hang your coat in the hall. Or would you prefer a glass of wine?'

'I would actually if you're having one.'

'I don't drink.'

'No?'

'But you go ahead.'

So I did. Well, this was novel. A teetotaller!

'How long have you been on your own Al?'

'Eighteen months. Eighteen long terrible, months!'

'I'm sorry about that. It does get easier with time though. And anyway, men I think, find it harder to cope.'

'Well, if the children were here, I would be distracted but I'm on my own for the most part.'

'I feel I was fortunate to have them all around me in the bad times. They certainly kept me going. How many do you have?'

'Three boys. All in London. Living the dream. And you?'

'Four girls and one boy. Only Erin at home now though. They grow up so fast.'

We talked about life and the simple things. Likes, Dislikes.

Al liked music, food, travel.

Well, that was safe enough I thought.

'We should go out some evening next week for dinner. I know a great place in Moycullen. Would you come with me?'

'Another date Al?'

'Ya, why not? If you want to that is.'

'Ok I'll come.'

We made small talk for a while and then I had to go.

There was no goodnight kiss. No handshake.

Time enough for that.

As he closed the door after me, he was a little less lonesome and a little more happy.

'Nice,' he thought.

I hadn't accepted his offer of a lift home as it was a fine night and I liked to walk. Home was close enough.

The week passed by the same as any, except I was looking forward to dinner at the Green Gables. I hadn't been there since the time of Jack.

We had chosen Saturday night as Al had to work late on Friday night.

He picked me up in his Land Rover.

'Nice,' I thought.

He was prompt and on time.

He was dressed in jeans and a pin stripe jacket. He believed in dressing for dinner.

I wore a blue dress and leather jacket with heels and a scarf. Very Maeve Binchy!

It was October and the winter had arrived.

'Aren't you cold?' I asked him.

'No not really.'

I discovered early on he was never cold.

Winter or summer he wore the same amount of clothes except a heavier jacket when there was snow and ice.

Jack on the other hand was always cold. It's what came from working in the desert for so many years.

Everything about the restaurant was top class.

'That's why we came this far,' he said.

'Oh? I thought you just wanted the safe distance between here and home?'

'Well, it's easier to talk when you go somewhere no one knows you.'

'That's true.'

'Otherwise you have to have a conversation with everyone you know. That's not the point of this date.'

'True.' I replied.

We talked about everything.

Al was inclined to talk about his late wife.

I decided that it was best to let him do that if it meant it would make him feel better.

He asked to meet up again the following week and I accepted. I liked his company. He was mature and very attractive.

We went to a different restaurant the following Saturday night in the opposite direction.

'Still trying to hide me?' I joked as I got into his car.

'Well, just for now,' he said.

'That's fine by me.'

'I have no wish to meet anyone I know right now.'

Again he picked a first-class restaurant. The Arch and River.

'Don't be worried about my reputation Al. I don't actually care about what people say.'

We had steak. True to his word he liked his food, all three courses. I opted for the main with wine.

When he was dropping me off, he kissed my cheek. Nice warm kiss. Nice warm lips.

I didn't exactly float home. More 'pepped in my step' home. If you get me.

The floating came later in the courtship.

Anyway we texted each other daily. I visited a couple of times a week. By now the rumour mill had kicked in, I guess, so I decided to tell the children.

Starting with Audrey.

'Oh mum. That's so cool. I'm delighted for you. Sure I know Al well. He's great. He would be so good for you.'

Chris was thrilled I was dating Al.

As far as Erin was concerned, I could do no wrong anyway, so she was happy.

Telling Cora was tricky. You see she was married herself, and 'Al and me as a couple' still had to pass muster with them both, I guess.

Cora took the engineer's route.

'Well, if you're happy and the chemistry is right, I couldn't be happier for you.'

And finally Finn. The only man in my life for years. He can be very witty and pithy. Nail on the head, in a funny, humorous sort of way. But not on this occasion. I couldn't remember when we had such a long conversation. It was great just to sit there in the inner sanctum of his bedroom, chatting.

He posed all the right reasons for dating. And why he thought I thought Al was such a good choice.

So I felt a whole lot more comfortable when I knew the troops were on my side.

When I told Al what I had done... bearing in mind it took a couple of weeks to get around to them all, he was relieved. They were living away so I had timed my information sessions when they visited. Nothing like the face-to-face conversations. They, and I, appreciate that when important issues have to be aired and decided on.

He was happy that they had accepted him. I don't think he could have dealt with rejection at that point.

Such a different reaction from his family. They didn't want to know. We have all become great friends in the meantime.

We were seeing each other for a couple of months when the relationship cranked up a notch.

We had been dating for a while. We hadn't progressed beyond the goodnight kiss or the occasional hug.

We had been out somewhere or other, probably the cinema. Arriving back at my house he got out to open the door for me. He gave me such a passionate kiss and hug that completely took my breath away. That never happened to me before. With anyone! He actually took my breath away. So it does happen.

'Will you stay with me tonight?

'I can't.'

'Why not? Finn is home. He will be with Erin.'

'Ok, I'll call him and organise it.'

I don't know what came over me.

Must have been the chemistry that Cora was on about before.

I chatted with Finn.

'Sure, no problem mum. See you in the morning.'

'Well, that was easy.'

I told Al.

So we headed back to his place.

I really didn't know what to expect.

'Why am I staying with you?' I asked like some idiot.

'I don't want to be alone anymore,' was all he said. 'Neither do I', I replied.

So we sat and chatted.

'Tell you what Al, if we are going to sleep together, we might as well do it tonight.'

'Yeah, I suppose you're right. I think we would make a good team.'

'Not so fast mister,' I thought to myself. 'I'm nobody's team.'

So we did it that night. Every fibre of my forty-something body came alive for the first time in a long time. Suffice it to say Al was magic. And still is.

The details are probably unimportant to anyone except myself.

So now, what do you think about the question, 'Is there such a thing as Mr Right?'

It's not that he was just great in bed mind you. That is not his only claim to fame. You have to know him to actually get him. He is steady. He is funny. He is handsome. He puts up with me. He gets me. Maybe not in the way Jack got me. Gerry was a great person. He loved life. It's tragic he lost it so soon. Jack loved his home-coming but didn't get to enjoy it for long.

I'm hoping myself and Al will get to grow old together.

That would be something.

Well, he thinks we are a good team so I couldn't resist taking his hand.

I know my mother would have approved.

Which is something to say.

My family love him. He came into my life at just the right time. As I said before.

I was an emotional fish for years and he sparked something in me which constituted a real awakening. He thawed me out. I keep him cool.

How could I not love the man?

'Yes, Cora the chemistry is fiiiiine.'

I am hoping there will be no more opportunities to investigate some other man as Mr Right. But you can see how I have had this question hanging over my head for decades.

If I can't answer now, how could I have hoped to have answered it at eighteen?

I wish with all my heart that life could have been simpler for me but that was not the case. And yet with each and every romance I was hooked.

Sceptics would say, 'you should a, would a, could a…'

Feck the sceptics.

Al would kill me for using the bad language even though he has the first-class degree in that discipline.

('What a Difference a Day Makes?' Dina Washington, 'It's heaven when you find romance on the menu': as the song goes. I love that he's part of my life.)

When I was on my own, I took my children wherever they needed to go. Naturally I drove them everywhere for years.

When I went out with Al at first, he drove. I would look across at the driver's side and thought.

Yes!

A man's leg.

The strength of that image comforted me.

The strength of that realisation settled me.

Something that simple.

Finally!

So we dated for a while and every so often I had to go to gymnastics competitions around the country with Erin. Overnight stays if the distance was too great to drive back again afterwards.

Al and I rarely met on Saturday night or Sunday night. But as time went on, I would have liked to see him every night.

We met several times every week and I usually stayed late.

Occasionally I stayed the night if there was someone at home with Erin.

After a while he started talking about getting married and to be honest, I preferred that option over living together or commuting between houses as it would have meant more stability for Erin. I had to think of her too. This wasn't all about me and Al having a lovely time. There was a minor child involved. So we did as the popular Paul Simon song says…

We were… 'lovers and married our fortunes together.'

Everyone was happy for us. The older children were especially so as they did not want their 'mammy' being on her own when they had all moved away. It wasn't really that basic, but they were just very happy for both of us. They all liked Al a lot. All mine that is.

His boys however went ballistic. I mentioned this already.

For months they would not speak to him even though they were all in relationships and living outside of Ireland.

They came home occasionally and were very vociferous in their opposition to the relationship. Not to me you understand but to the whole idea of 'daddy' being 'unfaithful' to his late wife. Well, I can hardly blame them.

But the guy was struggling to keep body and soul together. I had to take care of him. He was lost on his own and spent quite some time at the early stages of our relationship talking fondly about her. All part of the grieving process. I helped him through the hard times of grief.

I took the jumps with him.

Why not?

I loved him.

It was in our best interests.

Chapter 9

(Let me talk a bit about retirement.)

Well, if I wasn't already in boredom mode, from years of classrooms, not the students you understand, but the sameness of the curriculum, which had me practically lulled to a near narcoleptic state by the end, so giving up eight hours a day of some type of activity to a static lifestyle, nearly killed me. Always being one who showed up for work half hour early, I couldn't handle the 'lie-ins' as many of my ex-colleagues relished after they had downed tools.

Oh no.

Not me. I was so hotwired for most of my life to responsibility and 'up with the birds' that I narrowly avoided the nervous breakdown.

What, you might ask is the difference between a nervous breakdown and a state of 'full on depression'? I had already experienced the latter. Remember?

Well, there's a big difference. To my mind anyway.

Namely, having come through depression years earlier I was equipped enough to not let myself have a nervous breakdown.

You see depression is mental and is a progression so far as I can see. A nervous breakdown can happen quickly and be very physical, in a mental sort of way.

Also, depression is a condition where one is looking inward, whereas a breakdown is a jolt, something one is totally unprepared for. Not so much about self. Not so much about being consumed with oneself. A result of extrinsic conditions being almost insurmountable.

I was not prepared for that jolt, you understand. However, I know if I stayed at the job I was doing, I would have been a sure candidate for depression. Not that I would let myself slide so far again, knowing what I knew, but I was very hard put to be as happy at my job as I had been down through the years.

Maybe I just had some real desires I needed to pursue, like writing a book. A 'bucket list' if you like. But for all intents and purposes, I was challenged.

Challenged when I was in my later years at work. And challenged when I had retired.

I don't think I'm the only one in this boat, however, and maybe someone reading this might take solace in the fact there is life after retirement. I do believe I have come out the other end, but only just, and fairly recently.

For the first time in nearly two and a half years I am relaxed. Finding the niche that I need to be in for me.

A lot of people I worked with moved out of education and moved into jobs related to their previous work. Not so for me. Although I did try this route too you understand. But it's not for me anymore. I come out in a rash when I see a school uniform. Basically I spent thirty odd years buying them, washing them on Saturdays, ironing them on Sunday nights and then enforcing school uniform rules Monday to Friday. You can only take so much of the one ingredient or food group before you want to throw it up. Try it.

I didn't want to teach anymore.

I schooled my five offspring. I sent them out each morning. Collected them every evening. Sat with them as they did homework in the formative years. Drove them to their exams. Made coffee when they were flagging physically. Helped them to select their college courses. Encouraged them in their decisions. Empathised with them when they changed their minds. Cried silent tears when they went to live away.

All by myself.

While I held down a full-time teaching job.

And took on higher degrees and diplomas and such.

So eventually I had enough.

Not of them, you understand. The years of raising my children were the happiest years of my life.

I felt I didn't need to be fighting with the unruly offspring of other people.

At least I could unleash mine on the world and they were capable of saying 'please' and 'thank you'.

I thank my parents for that. They brought us all up with a sense of respect for other human beings as well as ourselves. If I could see her now and tell her that, I would be so happy.

My mother was special. She was refined. My dad was mannerly and refined. They were good parents.

So that is what I inherited.

And Jack helped me to understand my own children as persons in their own right.

There's an awful lot of amazing teenagers in the world.

I must say for the most part, I was blessed. But I grew out of the job. I reached as far as I could go on the promotion ladder. My head was hitting the roof of limited movement. I had to 'break free' as Freddie Mercury would say, although he probably penned that one for entirely different reasons.

I'm not ambitious but I am so in love with a challenge.

I just wasn't challenged enough to stay there.

So I initiated another challenge.

I have to say the hardest thing I have ever done in my life is 'nothing'.

And I have survived that too.

I was talking to my newly single, divorced friend the other night and I was reminded of the times I had to take a forty-foot Wavin plastic pipe to my septic tank to unblock my toilets. And then I was reminded of all the times I had to work on the air lock in my heating system and take a key to my radiators to let the air out of them so that they would actually work.

Lovely memories… but I had actually forgotten those episodes in my life until I was chatting with her. Now she is going through similar situations in her life while her 'off the hook', estranged other half is living the high life.

I also learned down through the years of singularity to change oil in my car, fix a faulty radiator in my car with an egg, put anti-freeze in my radiator in wintertime, coolant in the summertime, change a wheel, change a tyre, turn off the water at the mains, switch off the fuse box, switch the fuse box back on, change a plug, yadda-yadda-yadda! Never needing a man. I serviced my own washing machine, tumble dryer, dishwasher, boiler…

So I'm fully confident about her and all the rest of the competent women I know. As you may have guessed I didn't have time down through the years for the 'whinging ladies society' so I don't have now either, you understand.

The 'Oh my God' crew.

Women, generally, are cleverer and more capable than they realise.

Unless you have decided to be the damsel in distress. God help us.

You will cordially and willingly be rescued for some; what is known nowadays as 'booty.'

Good luck with that my fellow damsels.

Bearing in mind I have now been married three times.

Honestly, there is nothing they can do that we women cannot.

Well, they're physically stronger.

And yet I like to have their company!

I had six brothers who probably had six friends, so I get along with men, as I said.

If you find yourselves single in this hostile world, consider it an opportunity to better yourselves so that when Mr Right or Mr Right Now comes along you can happily eyeball him and say, 'really'?

Some will be so convincing by their flowers and dinners and opening doors and a kiss on the cheek.

Forget it.

The acid test is when he says, 'So do you have enough fuel for the winter?'

How many messages is he sending out right there and then?

Like you never think about these things, because you have never done it, because you only have been the sole provider, fixer, and enforcer, light for your family for years. Ya!

So, much as we women like flowers, we like the companionship even more.

It's all about turf or coal or gas or oil or whatever.

'Cos that's what your life has always been about.

Functionality.

Let it be so.

Not Friday night eighties or Saturday night disco but every day simple.

Yet he still does the flowers and hugs my children when they come to see us.

That and other stuff.

Icing on the cake.

Some time back the champion Formula 1 race driver Michel Schumacher took a fall when skiing off-piste and hit his helmeted head on a rock.

The helmet actually saved his life but it shattered on impact. That incident dragged my mind back to that hospital room of Morgan, as reports were circulated that the driver was on life support and his family were at his bedside and that his life was held in the balance.

Of course all I could think of was my absent brother Morgan. That's what happens and that's what always will happen when I hear similar stories. I will be back in that hospital room and will be breathing in that hospital-hushed atmosphere all over again.

Every time that East 17 Christmas song is played at Christmas time, I'm in my car driving to that hospital bed on Christmas day having settled my children in with their cousins. Not a Christmas goes by but I don't think about Jack. Jack being sick, Jack dying. East 17. And yet I love the song for its lyrics and the thoughts that were going through my head the first time I heard it on the way to the hospital after discovering he was terminal.

'Stay another day.'

'I've only just begun to know you.'

Despite the fact we were together for years.

There are other triggers too. Funerals in general take me back.

And movies like 'The Day After Tomorrow.'

Watching history channels when the air raid sirens sound.

News which shows the terror on children's faces as they are confronted with war and displacement.

So when asked by Mr Suit if I believed in Mr Right, I answered with an answer which went something like this...

'Absolutely. But for some people, maybe not everything is as cut and dried as it is for others...'

Chapter 10

I'm going to get personal her for a moment.

I was stricken with the menopause when I was exactly forty-nine. No warning. No lead in. One day I was functioning as I always have. The next I was another person altogether. Not recognising myself. I became a sniffling mess. I did not like myself at all.

(A warning to the faint hearted, maybe you should skip this chapter.)

It's fairly gruesome in a mental sort of way. Like I said there was no warning shot. No peri-menopause which could/should last for years and ease a person in. Not me however. At forty-nine years and one day it started and it was all over. All menstrual activity ceased. I toughed it out for about three months.

I think I first gave in to the new feelings, mental, emotional and physical when I was at a work-related seminar concerning drug information sessions for schools and getting to know the expert proposed to head up these seminars when I thought, 'that's it, I'm going to my G.P. to get drugs myself.' H.R.T. Ooh bad girl Cathy!

Ironic I know, but I was struggling with the symptoms.

I liken the advent of the menopause in my life to being hit by a runaway train. One day I was a Mrs High Achiever, multi-tasking successful parent and the next, a complete wreck of a person, derailed with a capital 'D' like the opening scenes of the movie, 'The Fugitive.' A freaking total mess. Excuse the hyperbole!

My whole life had to be put on hold whenever I was having a hot flush which was happening on the hour every hour or oftener. I'm sure millions of women have had similar experiences. But in the job I was doing, which required much concentration, I could only concentrate on the out of body experience of those hot flushes which were happening so regularly, and eventually drove me into the arms of my doctor. (Euphemistically speaking, that is.)

Well, his clinic at least.

He cautioned me.

I heard what he had to say.

Then, I'm afraid to admit, I nearly begged.

He recommended alternative treatment. Alternative. Black cohosh! Such a man reaction.

I stared him down.

He relented thankfully.

(Where did we hear that before?)

After a few weeks of medication I was back to normal, but I resented the fact that I had to rely on a drug to cope.

I never had to rely on drugs in my life even in the worst times and I prided myself on that fact. Yet here I was popping a pill every morning so I wouldn't go berserk from hot flushes or lack of sleep at night from the hot one minute, cold another minute phenomenon. And my brain was doing flip flops round the clock!

(My mad cow tablets I call them.)

I call the Menopause 'nature's cruellest trick of all'.

No question.

Yet I got used to what I had to do to be the stable normal person that I was pre-Menopause.

'So what is the significance,' I hear you say, 'of telling you about this episode in my life?'

'Episode' could be quantifiable. This was and is relentless, as I have at several times in the last number of years tried to cope without drugs. I usually manage for a month or so when I hurry to the drugstore to get my fix of 'mad cow' tablets.

I have dealt with grief. It's formulaic for me now. But I had to move through a lot more different emotions and feelings to get past the rebellion my body was and is putting me through since the onset of the mid-life crisis.

I haven't actually seen that production of 'My Funny Menopause' but I suspect the writer got off lightly at most or hasn't at any point experienced any of the harsh realities of reproductive life I had.

I know I wouldn't be humourizing or musicalizing about it. I see nothing funny about it whatsoever.

To all of you who are just setting out on the first stages of the same natural phenomenon, bless you, you'll get through it.

Some people can't take the drugs but there are other substances which can be 'tried.'

I still don't know if I should but it's a damn sight more comfortable than without for now.

Chapter 11

How can I put this down and end here. I cannot. I have to give some time to the wonderful people who have taken this journey with me for the most part.

They have been with me now nigh on thirty-eight years give or take a couple of years, depending on their birth dates.

Through thick and thin they have endured what I have endured, enjoyed what I have enjoyed, laughed when I laughed, cried when I cried. They are fearless individuals and have come through some very emotional times, and hard times. They are strong and have backbone. They have a sense of respect for everyone regardless of background or race. They have strong family bonds with their extended family.

My 'brood of chicks,' now 'fledgelings,' have flown the nest and are independent of me now.

It happened so fast, I find it hard to believe sometimes. One minute they were all around me taking up all my waking hours with their usual childhood lives, the next minute they are off doing their own lives.

I'm not mad about the 'empty nest syndrome' but I am well pleased about their resilience and their achievements.

Being a mother is so fulfilling but when they leave, they leave a great chasm which nothing can fill. They have travelled, lived abroad, came home, travelled again to such an extent it's hard to keep up with them. But I'm glad they did and they probably will again. It makes them broad minded and curious and adventurous and confident.

As parents we only get them for a short while and then they walk their own lives. It's rewarding, it's challenging.

Cora, the oldest, was four and a half when her father died. She had just started school in a very reputable rural school. I used to walk her to school most mornings and sometimes my neighbour would take the others to mind while I did. Mrs Hughes kindly obliged in the evenings as well. Where would we be without the help of other people?

Occasionally Gerry would still be at home in the mornings to take her and that was nice for them both. He bought and sold animals as a living and work took him away for very long days, so I was mostly at home on my own. Which was fine! I had developed a good routine and some days I went to visit my parents where I would meet up with all the in-laws and nieces and nephews. The younger generation loved to spend time and play with their cousins and it was all very wholesome and simple. Back then there was no technology and they spent hours playing out of doors winter and summer. They did the same things we did as kids, played in the haystacks, fished for 'jarogs' in the nearby stream, played hide and seek in the hay barn. What a 'great outdoors' type of start in life.

I did the jobs I had usually done when I was growing up for my mom. Cleaning, washing, cooking, shopping. Helping her cope.

It was lonesome back then too.

We both were.

But my marker was Cora. The most beautiful child in all humanity.

Only thing is she was forcibly delivered. At nine and a half months. Breech. Eight and a half pounds of a bum first, head last, never mind the mammy style delivery.

Anyway we survived.

I think this is why I was able to convince my family doctor years later that he should give me contraceptives. Had he delivered Cora safely I might not have actually been so close to death. And he knew that too.

So for the next couple of years Cora and I were seeing an Orthopaedic surgeon because she couldn't move her arms as a result of that injury received at birth. Thank God for my sis-in-law who put me wise to the situation.

Looking at her in a cot in the hospital at three months did nothing for my maternal instincts. My sister-in-law called it, I was too young and innocent to realise what was going on.

And then there were years of physiotherapy. Splints every day for months, until she could actually move her arms but only after she had shock treatment on her shoulder nerves at the orthopaedic ward.

Years later she played volleyball at national level for her school. Yet she has trouble brushing the back of her hair. She is a brilliant swimmer but can't backstroke. That's Cora.

She went to school at four and a half. She was in a lovely country school until her dad died and then she had to make so many changes.

Back at my mother's, she had to go to the local school, then she had to change again when we moved into the town. She never complained, fair play to her. She just liked school.

Thankfully. And there was never a negative comment about her from any teacher from day one. Only praise.

Being the eldest she led the way in everything. First at school. First to drive. First to go to college. First to leave home. First to go to another country to work. I spent my life saying goodbye to Cora. She married young. Happy girl. I could have done with a few more years of mommy/ Cora time. But then again I married young. History repeating itself.

Fair play to her she did a Doctorate. Completed it after months of a commute from London to her workplace. Two hours each way. One way to pass the time.

No one can diminish any of Cora's achievements. She's an achiever for sure.

But so are the others.

Take Chris for example. A write-off at secondary school, she had the infamous curse of tonsillitis which required back-to-back anti-biotics. Necessitating long absences from school, requiring her to drop down from higher level to ordinary level subjects, Chris had and has infinite internal resources and strength of will when it comes to picking oneself up.

She made so many supreme efforts of will to get where she is today. She felt the death of Jack so profoundly too that her life was a compendium of struggles. Starting with the death of her natural father Gerry, she had to accommodate two younger siblings from infancy. She is the most sociable baby I had. At sixteen months talking, swearing but not walking, could have a full-on conversation with me from an early age. Her communication skills are second to none. Chris does not suffer fools gladly.

I'm proud of her for that.

When the war started in The Middle East in Nineteen Ninety-One, she broke her arm. Dreaded boot skates as I said earlier. So we came home and then she re-broke it and had to go to the casualty department of the local hospital to have it reset, this time she had to have a pin inserted in her arm.

And had a cast for two months instead of six weeks. All the while missing out on the fullness of what the education system had to offer in this country.

Later on and undeterred by life's badly dealt hand Chris spent two years in Sydney. I always say you can't beat travelling. The more travelling mine did, the better, I thought. Gets the small-town mentality out of you and broadens your horizons. Makes you realise you can do whatever you want and be whatever you want. She came back with determination.

Subsequently she went to college and did a commerce degree and got herself a first-class Master's degree in business information systems.

Chris, the written off one!

And then there's Audrey. Born thirteen months after Chris, she was and is the most sociable of people. I guess being very busy with two other children didn't afford her the time she needed to vocalise all that was within her as an infant. However, we muddled through anyway and have reached a real open stage in our relationship. Audrey, uncommonly beautiful as a baby, and a stunning adult loved the bit of fun. She was all curls and comedy and people loved her right away for her outgoing personality.

After a couple of years it seemed as if I had triplet girls. They were very similar in looks and height. Audrey having grown a lot in the meantime measured up to them in no time at all.

(I had Finn also, but he was unmistakably a boy.)

Audrey was the flashy one. She was the most chatty one also and was very popular. I often thought that she would be an actress or a stand-up comedienne. She has a superb singing voice and is a brilliant artist. She is gifted creatively. She has an amazing intelligence about her concerning fashion and art and music.

Not especially sporty. Chris and Erin are the sporty ones.

Audrey could be a writer but she allowed herself to be talked into doing the wrong subjects at school and at the time I didn't have the expertise I do now to counteract that advice.

She headed off to Sydney when she was just turned nineteen. She spent two years there excelling at whatever it was she turned her hand to working and attending night school, learning Italian and such.

She loved being away. She loved the travelling. She eventually returned home, and after searching around for her niche for a few years she finally found it studying history at Trinity College, Dublin. Loving every minute of it. At least she got to go to Trinity. I am so proud of her. She is still cute and although her hair is not curly at all now, she is still comic. No matter what life has thrown at her she can still see the funny side. I could quote her ad infinitum but I won't. Her favourite phrase and mine is one of her own; 'paranoia is total awareness.'

You won't put anything past Audrey.

As a baby, Finn was one of the quietest infants I have ever known. He never needed discipline. He never did anything needing checking. He was an unusually well-behaved teenager. Was absolutely no trouble to his mother... Ever!

He was a nine-pound baby and required very little effort to raise. He ate and slept and amused himself. He did have the added advantage of Audrey who doted on him from day one. Cora and Chris were also very mindful of him but Audrey was his mainstay. They are the same to this day. The best of friends.

At that point, I had determined that my family was finished and as a non-working parent I had my own little crèche and so they amused each other while I took care of the chores and them.

When Finn was twenty months, his father died. He had measles at the time. Hi sisters had had them. Cora had brought it home from school. It was their first illness of any kind. They were impeccably healthy up until then.

Measles vaccination wasn't required as it is now.

I often wonder how each one of them, at their age then, felt the loss of their father. Nowadays they say they have no recollections of it, apart from Cora. How many of us remember as adults what was happening when we were four or just gone four?

Audrey was three and insists she has vivid memories.

Finn, obviously has none.

He travelled to Saudi with the rest of us when he was four and a half. He was nonplussed about that too as with most things. Not disconcerted at all that is.

He was very self-contained and could amuse himself for hours building Lego or reading a book or playing with his action figures. Mostly he liked things he had to assemble. He probably inherited his engineering skills from his uncles who like to strip down cars and reassemble them again.

He was fairly good at forming and keeping friendships although he wasn't one for sports. His favourite sporting activity was swimming. Outside of that he hadn't much time for field sports.

He was a little disappointed when Erin turned out to be a girl. He had his heart set on a brother. But he accepted her earnestly enough when the initial wave of disappointment had passed over. I think it lasted about a day.

After returning from Saudi, he settled back seamlessly to life in Ireland and to the Irish education system.

He made friends again and just got on with it. He made student of the year and went to college to do engineering. He loves his baby sister Erin and his older sisters too. He now has a daughter of his own and is a very capable father and loving husband. They spent some time in Canada, a place they love.

One would wonder sometimes how some people seem to take things in their stride so well. He hasn't had the easiest of lives but he has always maintained that calm which is his constant trait.

Erin was literally born in a warzone but she is as calm as her older brother. She wasn't a great sleeper unlike her older siblings. She needed to be around the whole time. Having an acute natural curiosity I would say she is one of the most prolific readers I know. Now her siblings are avid readers but the number of words that girl can consume in a day is unreal. And the type of books she used to buy for herself as teenager used to worry me. As soon as possible they were all given books to read regularly. A treat for them would be to get to go to the local bookshops in Either Saudi or Galway or London or wherever we were and make selections. Jack was brilliant for encouraging them to read. I believe it's the key to success. But her favourite haunt in all Ireland is not the high street shops, but Charlie Byrnes bookshop in Galway. It's an Aladdin's cave for her. Being stuck sometimes for gift ideas for her it will always come down to a Charlie Byrne's voucher.

So she reads a lot.

She is a gifted musician.

She has a Higher Degree in Art from Trinity.

She has several All-Ireland medals and some world gold medals in Gymnastics.

She was a busy girl growing up. I guess sleep wasn't that important or necessary. She stayed busy.

I should have said at the outset that her father died when she was four. She was devastated. That didn't hold her back, mind you, and now she is happily employed doing what she does and lives away from home and is planning to travel soon to Australia for her own personal adventure.

That's us.

Done and dusted as they say.

Chapter 12

At last 'Why?'

Last November my best friend, Sid, died.

I didn't know if I was going to mention this but I feel I owe it to him, after all he was one of my older brothers. If I mentioned the others, I should mention him.

I never believed for a second that I would lose him, but it came from nowhere.

Alive one minute.

Dead the next.

Brain haemorrhage.

If my sense of humour deserts me for a moment it will be while writing this passage.

It is a type of Eulogy for them all.

Here one day.

Gone the next.

Sid was the one that wrote me letters when I lived in Saudi. He was the one who saw us off at airports and picked us up at airports and he was the one who travelled with me for the most part of my journey when Jack was sick.

Nick would have been there too, as would David but they had families and work that tied them to schedules.

Sid would phone me daily while we lived through the Gulf War. He would phone me to see if I needed anything after

Jack died and would come and visit and ask about the children, making sure we had everything we needed.

He had children himself later in life.

Ever an amazing parent, even to mine he was so calm all his life. I think Morgan's passing affected him deeply and he never vocalised it. He was very quiet and sad I think most of his life after that.

He looked after my parents when they were elderly and was uniquely happy when his own children came along. All of mine loved him tremendously.

I refuse to become morbid here because his life was all about giving. He retained his sense of humour all his life no matter what circumstances came his way.

Maybe that is why the 'Why?'

Or How?

Anyway that's the way it is.

That's the truth.

My younger brother David jokingly declared to me one day that Nick and I and himself are collectables.

I got a chuckle out of that.

'Why?' you might ask.

Well, on occasions such as *that,* one might as well try to retain a healthy sense of humour.

A relative at Sid's funeral was overheard asking the question, 'I wonder who will be next?'

Whether she meant my family or our extended family isn't clear but the fact that she was thinking it puts everything into perspective.

We only get today. We may as well enjoy it.

Reach out to others. Keep busy because it's good for the soul.

Do nice things you have been putting off.

Try to remain tranquil. Hold on to your serenity.

Walk.

You will know what to do. These are just some of my suggestions.

And always love your family.

Ingram Content Group UK Ltd.
Milton Keynes UK
UKHW020834140723
425125UK00012B/365

9 781035 809400